Quick Children's Sermons 4:

Did Samson Eat Spinach?

Group

Loveland, Colorado

Group's R.E.A.L. Guarantee to you:

This Group resource incorporates our R.E.A.L. approach to ministry—one that encourages long-term retention and life transformation. It's ministry that's:

Relational
Because learner-to-learner interaction enhances learning and builds Christian friendships.

Experiential
Because what learners experience through discussion and action sticks with them up to 9 times longer than what they simply hear or read.

Applicable
Because the aim of Christian education is to equip learners to be both hearers and doers of God's Word.

Learner-based
Because learners understand and retain more when the learning process takes into consideration how they learn best.

Quick Children's Sermons 4:
DID SAMSON EAT SPINACH?

Copyright © 2003 Group Publishing, Inc.

Credits

Contributing Authors: Linda A. Anderson, Sharon Carey, Teryl Cartwright, Sara K. Elder, Becca Koopmans, Julie Lavender, Elaine Ernst Schneider, and Donna K. Simcoe

Editor: Amy Nappa

Acquisitions Editor: Karl Leuthauser

Chief Creative Officer: Joani Schultz

Copy Editor: Dena Twinem

Book Designer: Jean Bruns

Cover Art Director: Bambi Eitel

Cover Illustrator: Liisa Chauncy Guida

Print Production Artist: Shelly Dillon

Production Manager: Peggy Naylor

Unless otherwise noted, Scripture taken from the HOLY BIBLE, NEW INTERNATIONAL VERSION®. Copyright © 1973, 1978, 1984 by International Bible Society. Used by permission of Zondervan Publishing House. All rights reserved.

Library of Congress Cataloging-in-Publication Data

Quick children's sermons 4 : did Samson eat spinich?
    p. cm.
Includes index.
ISBN 0-7644-2459-9 (pbk. : alk. paper)
1. Children's sermons. I. Title: Did Sampson eat spinach?. II. Group Publishing.
BV4315 .Q546 2002
252'.53--dc21
        2002011509

ISBN 0-7644-2459-9
10 9 8 7 6 5 4 3 2 1   12 11 10 09 08 07 06 05 04 03
Printed in the United States of America.

Contents

Introduction 6

Questions Kids Ask About the
OLD TESTAMENT

Who Made God? *(Genesis 1:1-2)* 8
Do I Really Look Like God? *(Genesis 1:24-28)* 10
Did God Take a Nap on the Seventh Day? *(Genesis 2:2-3)* 12
Did Adam Ever Get His Rib Back? *(Genesis 2:19-24)* 14
Why Didn't God Like Cain's Offering? *(Genesis 4:1-8)* 16
Did the Unicorns Miss the Ark? *(Genesis 6:11–7:5)* 18
Were There Rainbows Before the Flood? *(Genesis 9:8-17)* 20
Did the Tower of Babel Go All the Way to Heaven?
   (Genesis 11:1-9) 22
Was Abram Able to Count All the Stars?
   (Genesis 15:1-6; 22:17a) 24
Was Sarah As Old As My Grandma When She Had Isaac?
   (Genesis 21:1-7) 26
Why Was Esau So Hairy? *(Genesis 27:1-40)* 28
Why Didn't Joseph Just Share His Coat? *(Genesis 37:1-4)* 30
Do My Dreams Tell the Future Like Joseph's Dreams Did?
   (Genesis 37:5-10; 41:25-32) 32
Why Did Pharaoh Keep Changing His Mind About
   Letting the Israelites Go? *(Exodus 5–12)* 34
Why Did God Send All Those Plagues on Egypt?
   (Exodus 5–12) 36
What Did Manna Taste Like? *(Exodus 16:1-31)* 38
Was God Mad at Moses for Breaking the Tablets?
   (Exodus 32:1-20; 34:1-10) 40
Why Did the Israelites March Around the Wall of Jericho
   Seven Times? *(Joshua 6:1-20)* .42
Did Samson Eat Spinach? *(Judges 16)* 44
Why Can't I Hear God Like Samuel Did? *(1 Samuel 3:1-11)* 46
Did Goliath Live on a Beanstalk? *(1 Samuel 17)* 48
Why Was King Saul So Grumpy? *(1 Samuel 20)* 50

3

Why Didn't David Get Even With Saul When He Had
the Chance? *(1 Samuel 24)* 52
Was Solomon Smarter Than Jesus? *(1 Kings 3:1-15)* 54
Did the Ravens Bring Toys and Games to Elijah Too?
(1 Kings 17:1-6) 56
Was Esther Prettier Than Snow White? *(Esther 2)* 58
Were Shadrach, Meshach, and Abednego Superheroes?
(Daniel 3) 60
Did Daniel Get to Pet the Lions? *(Daniel 6)* 62
Did Jonah Get Seasick in the Whale? *(Jonah 1)* 64

Questions Kids Ask About the
NEW TESTAMENT

What Are Frankincense and Myrrh? *(Matthew 2:1-11)* 68
Did Jesus Have to Go to School? *(Luke 2:41-52)* 69
Why Did John the Baptist Eat Such Yucky Food?
(Matthew 3:1-12) 71
Why Were the Pharisees Always So Mean to Jesus?
(Matthew 22:15-22) 73
If Jesus Liked Children So Much, Why Didn't He Have Any?
(Mark 10:13-16) 74
Did Jesus Pick Up the Tables After He Knocked Them Over?
(John 2:12-25) 76
Why Did Jesus Tell So Many Stories? *(Mark 4:1-20)* 78
What Makes Jesus Laugh? *(John 1:1-14)* 80
Did Jesus Just Pretend to Be Asleep Before He Calmed
the Storm? *(Matthew 8:23-27)* 82
What Did Jesus Do With All the Leftover Food After He
Fed Five Thousand People? *(John 6:1-14)* 84
Did Jesus Walk on the Moon? *(Matthew 14:22-33)* 85
Did Everyone Like Zacchaeus After He Met Jesus?
(Luke 19:1-9) 86
Was Jesus More Popular Than My Favorite Music Group?
(Mark 2:1-12) 88
Why Did Peter Get Into So Much Trouble?
(Matthew 26:69-75) 90
Did God Forget About Jesus When He Was on the Cross?
(Mark 15:33-41) 92

Why Didn't Jesus Just Use His Power to Get Down
From the Cross? *(Luke 23:33-43)* 94
Does Jesus Still Have Holes in His Hands? *(John 20:24-31)* 96
Where Is Jesus Now? *(Acts 1:1-11)* 98
Is the Holy Spirit Inside of Me? *(Acts 2:1-13)* 100
Did Saul's Horses Go Blind Too? *(Acts 9:1-20)* 103
Why Is the Book of Revelation So Confusing?
(Revelation 21:1-7, 16-26; 22:1-3) 105

SCRIPTURE INDEX 107
THEME INDEX 107

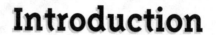

Introduction

What did manna taste like?
Did Daniel get to pet the lions?
Was Esther prettier than Snow White?

Kids ask some great questions! They always want to go deeper, asking questions that even adults might be wondering (but are too proud to ask out loud!). Adults and kids alike can learn from the straightforward, honest questions kids ask.

Children's questions provide a wonderful opportunity to dig into God's Word, talk about faith, and encourage kids' love for God. *Quick Children's Sermons 4: Did Samson Eat Spinach?*, the fourth book in this popular series, can help you make the most of that opportunity. Each quick sermon is based on Scripture and is created to keep kids' attention while encouraging their participation. And with the handy "Simple Supplies" list included with each sermon, anyone can present a meaningful message with minimal preparation.

You won't want to limit the use of these active messages to weekly worship. They're great for church-family gatherings, Sunday school teachers meetings, children's church, Sunday school, and midweek programs. Anyone who loves children will enjoy sharing these sermons with kids of all ages.

Quick Children's Sermons 4: Did Samson Eat Spinach? contains questions kids really ask. So gather the children, and have fun as you share God's truth by answering questions that come straight from the heart of the child in each of us!

Questions Kids Ask About the Old Testament

Who Made God?

THEME

God has always been here and always will be.

BIBLE REFERENCE
Genesis 1:1-2; Isaiah 43:10b; Revelation 1:8

SIMPLE SUPPLIES
You'll need a Bible, alphabet cards from A to Z, and both old and new pennies.

Who's the oldest person you know? What's the oldest object you own? *Allow children to respond.* Genesis 1:1-2 says, "In the beginning God created the heavens and the earth. Now the earth was formless and empty, darkness was over the surface of the deep, and the Spirit of God was hovering over the waters." When do you think the beginning was? *Allow children to respond.*

Hold up an old penny (the older the better). How old do you think this penny is? *Read the year on the penny to the children.* Name some things you know of that are older than this penny. *Allow children to respond.*

Have children each turn to someone and share their ages. How old do you think I am? *Allow children to respond. If you're willing, share your age.*

How old do you think God is? *Allow children to respond.*

Open your Bible to Revelation 1:8, and show the verse to the children. The Bible tells us how long God has existed. Here in Revelation 1:8 it says, " 'I am the Alpha and the Omega,' says the Lord God, 'who is, and who was, and who is to come, the Almighty.' " Alpha and Omega are the first and last letters of the Greek alphabet. What are the first and last letters in our alphabet? *Allow children to respond. Hold up the alphabet cards for the children to see. Give one alphabet card to each child.*

I want you to stand, hold your letter in the air, and say your letter of the alphabet when it's your turn. We'll start with A. OK, go! *Have each child stand in turn and say the alphabet according to the card he or she is holding. For a little extra fun, you could have the children repeat the activity by saying the alphabet backward.*

Note: If you have more kids than letters, have some or all children form pairs. If you have fewer kids than letters, let some children have more than one letter.

After the alphabet has been said, have children sit down. Who can tell me what letter comes before A? *Pause for children to answer.* There is no letter before A, just as there was nothing before God—he was always there.

Open your Bible to Isaiah 43:10b. Listen to what the Bible says in Isaiah

43:10: "Before me no god was formed, nor will there be one after me."

Not only has God always existed, but he always will exist! That means that he was there for your great-great-great-great-great-great-grandparents and he's here for you right now. And God will be there for your great-great-great-great-great-great-grandchildren—and even after that. Isn't that great?

When are some of the times you would want to know that God is with you? *Allow children to respond. As each child responds, reassure him or her that God will be there.* Aren't you glad God has always been there and always will be?

Let's pray together. ♥ Dear God, thank you for all the things in creation that you made. And thank you for always being there—in the past, in the future, and right now for us. You are an awesome God! Amen. ♥

I'm going to give each of you one old penny and one new penny as a reminder that God was there when the old penny was new and he'll still be there when the new penny is old.

Do I Really Look Like God?

THEME

Your heart can reflect God's image.

BIBLE REFERENCE

Genesis 1:24-28; 1 Samuel 16:7b; Proverbs 27:19; Ezekiel 36:26

SIMPLE SUPPLIES

You'll need a Bible, a picture of yourself as a child, a picture of your parents, and aluminum foil.

Hold up the picture of yourself as a child, and then hold up the picture of your parents. (If you have a multigenerational family in your church, you may want to ask them to volunteer to do this live.)

What similarities do you see in these people? *Allow time for children to look and answer.* Has anyone ever said to you, "You have your father's eyes" or "You have your mom's smile"? Who do you look most like? *Allow children to respond.* Most of the time, children look a little like their parents, but don't look exactly like them. That's kind of how it works with God and us.

Open your Bible to Genesis 1:24-28, and read the passage aloud. What do you think God looks like? *Allow children to respond.* Genesis 1:26 says, "Then God said, 'Let us make man in our image, in our likeness.' " Why do you think God wanted to make us like him? In what way do you think we look like God? *Allow children to respond.*

The Bible tells us that we were formed in God's image. That means that all of us look a little bit like God. But the better question is "How do our hearts look like God's heart?" You see, God isn't concerned with what we look like. In fact, the Bible tells us in 1 Samuel 16:7, "The Lord does not look at the things man looks at. Man looks at the outward appearance, but the Lord looks at the heart." What do you think your heart looks like to God? *Allow children to respond.*

If we let him, God will change our hearts to be more like his. He promised he would do that in Ezekiel 36:26. It says, "I will give you a new heart and put a new spirit in you; I will remove from you your heart of stone and give you a heart of flesh." God can do this for us.

What are some things people do that show they have a "new heart" that God gave them? What are some things that you can do to show your heart is like God's? *Allow children to respond.*

Let's look at another verse in the Bible that talks about how our hearts can reflect God. *Open your Bible to Proverbs 27:19.* This verse says, "As water reflects a face, so a man's heart reflects the man." Since our hearts reflect who we are, as this verse says, when we let God give us new hearts, we will reflect God. Isn't that great?

Let's pray together. ♥ Dear God, thank you that you love us so much that you would change our hearts to be like yours. Please give us new hearts that are more like yours so that we will reflect your image to others. Thank you, God. Amen. ♥

Let's make something now that you can take home with you as a reminder that it's your heart that reflects God's image. *Give each child a one-foot piece of aluminum foil. Have children roll the foil lengthwise and then form a "V" shape. After forming a "V" shape, have them curve each end inward to form a heart shape.* When you get home, take the heart shape and stand in front of a mirror. Place the heart up to your face and look in the mirror. When you do, ask God to help your heart reflect his image, just as the mirror reflects your face.

Did God Take a Nap on the Seventh Day?

THEME

God never sleeps, but always watches over us.

BIBLE REFERENCE
Genesis 2:2-3; Psalm 121:3b-4

SIMPLE SUPPLIES
You'll need a Bible, a globe, and pillow-shaped butter mint candies.

How many of you like to make things? What's the most difficult thing you've ever made? Does making things sometimes make you tired? What do you do when you're tired? *Allow the children to respond.*

The Bible tells us that God created everything in six days. That's a lot of things to create in just six days! How do you think God felt when he was finished with creation? What do you think God did when he was finished with his creation? *Allow children to respond.*

Let's read what the Bible says about what God did after he created everything. *Open your Bible to Genesis 2:2-3.* "By the seventh day God had finished the work he had been doing; so on the seventh day he rested from all his work. And God blessed the seventh day and made it holy, because on it he rested from all the work of creating that he had done."

God rested. What do you think God did when he rested? Do you think it means that God took a nap? Do you think God slept? Do you think God ever sleeps? *Allow the children to respond.* Let's take a look at what the Bible says about whether or not God ever sleeps.

Open your Bible to Psalm 121. Psalm 121 tells us about how God helps us and watches over us all the time. How do you think it's possible for God to watch over the whole earth all the time? *Allow children to respond.*

Have kids look at the globe. If possible, have kids stand and surround the globe. Allow children to respond to the following questions. Does everybody in the world sleep at the same time? What kinds of things do people all over the world do during the times they are awake? When people are awake, they do things like go to work, go to school, play, read books, cook meals, go shopping, and lots of other things. What do you think God does when people are doing all of these things?

Now let me read Psalm 121:3-4 to you. "He who watches over you will not slumber; indeed, he who watches over Israel will neither slumber nor sleep." What does that tell us about God sleeping? *Allow children to respond.* That's right. God never sleeps. He is watching over all of the people in the world because he loves us so much. And that means God is watching over you! God didn't need to take a nap after he made the world—God never gets tired. God was just showing us that he wants us to take time to rest.

Let's pray together. ❤ Dear God, thank you that we can trust you to always watch over us. We're so glad that you don't need to sleep and that allows you to watch over us and keep us safe. Thank you for your protection and for your rest. Amen. ❤

I have a small treat for you today, little candies that look like tiny pillows. *Give each child one of the pillow-shaped butter mint candies.* You can eat your candy right now as you think about God who watches over you and never sleeps.

Did Adam Ever Get His Rib Back?

THEME

When God takes something from us, we often receive something better in return.

BIBLE REFERENCE
Genesis 2:19-24; John 3:16-17

SIMPLE SUPPLIES
You'll need a Bible, mini marshmallows, and Rice Krispies treats.

Have children point to their ribs. How many ribs can you count? What do you think would happen if you lost one of your ribs? *Allow children to answer.*

Open your Bible to Genesis 2:19-24. The Bible tells us how God brought all of the birds and animals to Adam so he could give them names. How would you have felt if you'd been able to name everything? That's a pretty big job!

Give each child a marshmallow, but tell children that it's very important that they not eat them. I want you to pretend that you've never seen a marshmallow before. What would you name the object you're holding? *Allow children to respond.* It's very important that you not eat your marshmallows, because we're going to use them later. *Have children place their marshmallows on their laps until the end of your teaching time.*

Even with all of those birds and animals, Adam was still lonely. He didn't have anyone he could talk to and share things with. When are some times when you feel lonely? *Have children share with partners their answers to the question. Then describe a time you've been lonely. (By doing this, you'll help the children understand that everyone gets lonely sometimes—even adults.)*

God didn't want Adam to be lonely all the time, so he came up with a plan. Let's read about it. *Open your Bible to Genesis 2:20b-24.* Genesis 2:20-22 says, "But for Adam no suitable helper was found. So the Lord God caused the man to fall into a deep sleep; and while he was sleeping, he took one of the man's ribs and closed up the place with flesh. Then the Lord God made a woman from the rib he had taken out of the man, and he brought her to the man."

God made Adam's rib into a woman. Isn't that amazing? God took Adam's rib, but gave Adam something much better in return—a wife! What do you think Adam thought about getting a wife for his rib? *Allow children to respond.*

Let's read what Adam said when he saw the woman God made for him.

14

Genesis 2:23 reads, "The man said, 'This is now bone of my bones and flesh of my flesh; she shall be called "woman," for she was taken out of man.' " Do you think Adam was happy about getting a wife? Why or why not? *Allow children to respond.*

Have you ever had to give up something close to you to get something better? For example, let's say you had to give up having your own room, but you got a baby brother? *Allow children to respond.* It's not always easy to give up something that is important to you. Let's look at what God gave up for us.

Open your Bible to John 3:16-17. John 3:16-17 tells us, "For God so loved the world that he gave his one and only Son, that whoever believes in him shall not perish but have eternal life. For God did not send his Son into the world to condemn the world, but to save the world through him."

God gave up something even more special than Adam did. God gave up his Son, and in return he provided a way to have a relationship with the whole world. Because of sin, God couldn't have a relationship with us, but because of Jesus, he can. When we believe in Jesus, God can have that relationship with us again!

Now I have a surprise for you. I want all of you to come and give me your marshmallows, and I'll give you something else in return. *Have each child come up to you and give up his or her marshmallow. In return, give the child a Rice Krispies treat.*

Often, when God asks us to give up something, he gives us something better in return. Let's pray together. ❤ Dear God, thank you that you want to have a relationship with us and that because of that, you were willing to give up your Son, Jesus. We also thank you that we can trust you to provide for us when you take something away, just as you did for Adam when you took his rib and gave him a wife. Amen. ❤

Why Didn't God Like Cain's Offering?

THEME

God wants us to have attitudes that please him.

BIBLE REFERENCE

Genesis 4:1-8; Hebrews 11:4

SIMPLE SUPPLIES

You'll need a Bible, a picture your child (or a child from your group) has drawn for you, and a copy of a famous painting. (You can find a famous painting in an art book at the library.)

Hold up the picture your child drew. How much do you think this drawing is worth? What's special about this drawing? Why do you think it means so much to me? *Allow children to respond.*

Hold up the copy of the famous painting. How much do you think this painting is worth? What's special about it? Which do you think means more to me, my child's drawing or this painting? Why? *Allow children to respond.*

Although the original painting in this picture is beautiful and is very valuable, I cherish the drawing my child gave me because it was given with love.

Allow children to respond to the following questions. How do your parents react when you give them something you made especially for them? How does that make you feel? What are some of the special things you've given to your mom or dad? How did you feel when you were making them? How did you feel when you were getting ready to give something you made to your parents? It's exciting to give something special to someone we love, isn't it? Let's look at two brothers and the gifts they gave to God.

In Genesis 4:1-8 we learn about Cain's and Abel's offerings to God. Let's take a look at it. *Open your Bible to Genesis 4:1-8, and read the passage aloud.* Notice that the Bible says that Cain brought "some of the fruits of the soil as an offering to the Lord." But Abel brought the "fat portions from some of the firstborn of his flock."

Allow children to answer the following questions. What was the difference between what Abel offered and what Cain offered? Why do you think Abel gave his best to God? What do you think Cain was thinking when he gave his offering to God?

Abel brought the best of what he had and offered it to God because he loved God and wanted to give God the very best he had. Cain only brought some of the fruits of the soil as an offering. Notice that it doesn't say Cain brought his best fruits or his first fruits—he just brought some of his fruits. He wanted to give to God, but he didn't want it to cost him too much.

Open your Bible to Hebrews 11:4, and read the verse to the children. Why was Abel's offering to God a better sacrifice than Cain's? Because Abel gave to God out of a heart of love and Cain gave to God out of obligation, or because he felt like he had to. What are some things you can give to God? *Allow time for children to answer.* When you give to God because you love him and not because you have to, it makes God happy.

Let's pray together. ❤ Dear God, help us to always have attitudes that make you happy. Whenever we give you something, help us to do it because we love you and not because we feel like we have to. Thank you that because you loved us first, we can love you. Amen. ❤

Did the Unicorns Miss the Ark?

THEME

We should follow God's direction.

BIBLE REFERENCE
Genesis 6:11–7:5

SIMPLE SUPPLIES
You'll need a Bible.

What do you remember most about a man named Noah? *Let children respond.* I remember Noah as a man who knew how to follow directions.

Once God spoke to Noah with a long list of important directions. God explained that because the whole earth was full of sin and people were hurting each other, he was going to destroy it with a great flood. He told Noah to build a large boat to keep his family safe while the deep waters covered the earth. Because Noah loved God, he listened very carefully as God explained step by step how to build a big boat called an ark.

Are you good at following directions? When you're given a job, do you pay close attention to the instructions and then carefully follow them? *Let children respond.* Let's play a listening game. I'll give you several directions. Listen carefully to all of them, and then begin. *Give the children a set of three or four simple commands such as touch your nose, touch your toes, turn around, and sit down. When they have finished, give them another set of instructions but increase the number of actions involved.* The more directions I gave you, the harder it was to finish the job, but you all did very well.

To build the ark, Noah had to follow many directions. God told him exactly how tall, how wide, and how long the ark was to be. He told him what to build on the inside and how to cover the outside so that water wouldn't soak through. God told Noah where to put the windows and the door and how many different levels it should have. Noah wanted to do what God commanded, so when God spoke, Noah paid attention, and together they built the ark.

God not only told Noah how to build the ark, but he also told him what to put inside of it. *Open your Bible to Genesis 6:19.* God said, "You are to bring into the ark two of all living creatures, male and female, to keep them alive with you."

The Bible doesn't tell us how the animals came to the ark. Maybe Noah and his family gathered the animals, or maybe God called them and, just like Noah, the animals did as God said.

What kinds of animals came into the ark? *Allow children to respond.* There were thundering elephants, squawking chickens, squealing monkeys, and beautiful chirping birds. Every kind of animal was on the ark. No animal was left behind. Some people think that unicorns aren't around anymore because they didn't get onto the ark, but the Bible says that two of all living creatures got on the ark. Unicorns are really just imaginary animals, not creatures that got left behind in the flood.

It took Noah a hundred years to build the ark! When it was finally done and filled with Noah's family and the animals, it must have been a pleasing sight to God...and a noisy one! Let's imagine what it might have sounded like on the ark after all of the animals were on board. *Let the children choose animal sounds to imitate and make the room sound as if it were the ark.*

Open your Bible to Genesis 6:22. The story of Noah begins with God's important directions to Noah and mentions these important words, "Noah did everything just as God commanded him."

God probably won't ask any of you to build an enormous boat and fill it with a zoo, but he asks you to do other important things. *Let the children respond to the following questions.* What does God ask you to do? Where can you find God's directions? What directions does the Bible give you?

Learning to follow directions is an important lesson. Learning to follow *God's* directions in the Bible is the most important lesson of all. Decide that you will be like Noah and do as the Lord commands.

Let's pray. ❤ Dear God, help me to obey you as Noah did and learn to please you by following your directions. Amen. ❤

Close by giving your kids simple directions such as walking backward, or imitating an animal as they return to their seats.

Were There Rainbows Before the Flood?

THEME

God helps us remember his promises.

BIBLE REFERENCE

Genesis 9:8-17

SIMPLE SUPPLIES

You'll need a Bible; strips of construction paper in each of these colors: blue, yellow, green, red, and orange; and one snack-size bag of Skittles or M&M's candy for each child.

Before you begin, write "Rainbow Treats" on a self-adhesive note. I have a small gift that I'll give each of you at the end of our lesson. This note will be my reminder. *Let the children suggest where to place the note so you'll remember it.* When I see my note I'll remember my promise.

Reminder notes help us remember important things. God helps us remember important things too. Some of the most important things to remember are God's promises.

God helps us remember his promises. In fact, he did something very special to help us remember one of his promises. His reminder is better than a note on the refrigerator. It's bigger and brighter than anything marked on a calendar. It goes from one side of the sky to the other. Do you know what it is? *Let children respond.* You're right! Let's see how the rainbow is a reminder to us.

The Bible tells us about a time when the world was so full of sin that God covered it with water and destroyed every living thing. Only a man named Noah and his family believed God. They were kept safe in an ark that God commanded Noah to build.

After the flood was over, God made a promise. *Open your Bible to Genesis 9:13, 15b.* God said, "I have set my rainbow in the clouds, and it will be the sign of the covenant between me and the earth...Never again will the waters become a flood to destroy all life." This was the very first rainbow, and it came with a special promise!

Let's make a rainbow to help us remember God's promise. *Give each child one strip of colored paper.* As I read this poem, listen carefully and when you hear me say the name of your color, hold it up to make a rainbow.

The rain had stopped, the sky was *blue*, the dark clouds rolled away.

The *yellow* sun was shining down as Noah bowed to pray.

"Thank you, Lord, that you have brought us safely through the flood,

And made the earth grow *green* again and filled it with your love."

Then Noah heard a *red* bird sing and looked up toward the sky.

He saw the most unusual thing that ever caught his eye.

God set a rainbow up above for everyone to see.

It sent a message, big and bright: "Remember this," said he.

"The earth will never be destroyed with waters strong and deep,

This is a promise I have made and a promise I will keep.

Forget none of my promises; each one I've made is true,

I'll help you to remember them, *'orange'* you glad I do?"

What message is God helping us remember when he puts a rainbow in the sky? What other promises does God help you remember? *Let the children respond.*

Let's pray. ❤ Dear God, help us remember your promises and never forget that you keep each one. Amen. ❤

As you close, let the kids remind you of the note you set out earlier. Pass out the candies for the kids to take home and enjoy later. Each little bag contains some colors of the rainbow. As you eat each piece of candy, try to remember some of God's promises.

Did the Tower of Babel Go All the Way to Heaven?

THEME

Ignoring God is always a bad idea.

BIBLE REFERENCE

Genesis 11:1-9

SIMPLE SUPPLIES

You'll need a Bible, several travel magazines or brochures, and someone who speaks a foreign language.

What if you and your family had the whole earth to yourselves and could make your home anywhere you wanted? Would you live by the ocean, or on a mountaintop, or near a nice stream? *Pass out the travel pictures, and let the children look at them briefly as they respond.* As you can see, there are many wonderful places in our world to live. If you found a place you liked very much, what would you do? *Allow children to respond.*

After the flood, when Noah and his family stepped off the ark, they were the only ones on the earth. Everything was ready for a new beginning. God commanded Noah's family to scatter throughout the earth and begin to fill it again with new families.

Do you know what the word "scatter" means? Let's imagine that this room is the whole earth. Show me how you would scatter throughout the earth. *Allow children to move about the room for a few minutes, and then call them back.*

After awhile, the people decided that they did not want to scatter anymore. They found a nice place to live and decided to stay there. They ignored God's plan and made their own plan.

Open your Bible to Genesis 11:4. In Genesis 11:4, the Bible tells us what the people did. "Then they said, 'Come, let us build ourselves a city, with a tower that reaches to the heavens, so that we may make a name for ourselves and not be scattered over the face of the whole earth.' "

Why did the people build a city and a great, high tower? What was wrong with that idea? *Let the children respond.* The people were doing the very opposite of what God told them to do. They were so proud of themselves and the tower they built. They would gather at the tower, look up to the top, and think about how great they were to have built such a thing. They didn't want to ever leave it. But they would soon learn that ignoring God is never a good idea. God decided to put a stop to the tower and the

22

city and do something that would cause the people to scatter.

I've invited a friend to tell us what God did. *Ask your guest to read Genesis 11:7-9 in another language.*

What was our friend saying? How did it feel to suddenly not understand what you were hearing? *Let the children respond.* Listen as I read the same verses our friend just read. *Read Genesis 11:7-9.* The name Babel means confused. God confused the language of the people so that they had to separate into groups. They moved away from the city and the tower they thought reached all the way to heaven.

Did the Tower of Babel reach all the way to heaven? Imagine the tallest building you've ever seen. *Have the children pretend to look up toward the top of a skyscraper.* When you stand at the bottom you can barely see the top. Today our cities have skyscrapers that are much taller than the Tower of Babel, but in Bible times, it was the tallest thing anyone had ever built.

It would have been so much better if the people had obeyed God instead of ignoring his command. Just like the people at the Tower of Babel, we sometimes want our own way instead of God's way, but ignoring God is always a bad idea. What happens when people ignore God? When do you feel like ignoring God? What should you do when that happens? *Let the children respond to each question.*

Let's pray. ❤ Dear God, keep me from going my own way. Help me to never ignore your commands but to obey you every day. Amen. ❤

Was Abram Able to Count All the Stars?

THEME

Trust God, no matter what.

BIBLE REFERENCE
Genesis 15:1-6; 22:17a

SIMPLE SUPPLIES
You will need a Bible, a piece of black paper and a brightly colored gel pen for each child, an overhead projector, a solid sheet of paper with many tiny holes poked into it, and a cup of sand spread onto a cookie sheet.

Do you like to count? Are you pretty good at it? I wonder if you would help me count something. *Bring out the cookie sheet with the sand.* Would you count these grains of sand? *Let children count for a minute, then ask for the number.* I think this job's too difficult for us! *Put the sand aside.* Even the best counters in the world would have a hard time counting each and every tiny grain of sand here. Did you know that God once asked a man to try to count something as impossible as that?

The Bible tells us about a man named Abram. He had many servants and great riches, but there was one thing he did not have. Abram had no children. God had promised Abram and his wife that they would have a son. *Open your Bible and read Genesis 22:17a.*

One day there would be so many children in Abram's family that no one would be able to count them. His family would eventually become a whole nation! That was a wonderful promise from God, but as Abram grew older and older, he still had no children. How do you think Abram felt as he waited? *Allow children to respond.*

Open your Bible to Genesis 15:5a. One night, God took Abram outside. Genesis 15:5 says, "He took him outside and said, 'Look up at the heavens and count the stars—if indeed you can count them.' " When Abram looked up into the sky, what do you think he saw? *Place the perforated sheet of paper on the overhead, and focus it on the ceiling.*

Have you ever seen the sky on a clear night when many stars are shining brightly? Was Abram able to count all the stars? Can anyone? *Allow children to respond.* Only God, who created our universe, knows how many stars fill the sky.

Abram couldn't count all the stars. But God promised Abram that someday he would have so many people in his family that to count them would be like trying to count every tiny speck of light in the night sky or every grain of sand on the seashores. Abram had to trust God that this promise would come true.

When is it hard for you to trust God? What can you do to show that you are trusting God no matter what? *Let children respond.*

Give each child a sheet of black paper and a gel pen. Use the overhead projector to show the children how to draw a simple five-line star.

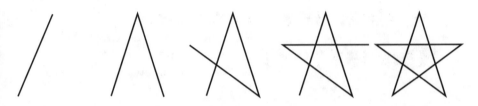

As we draw each line of the star, let's say a word from our lesson. *Say the following words as you draw each line of the star.* Trust—God—no—matter—what. Whenever you look up into the night sky and see it filled with stars, remember that when we trust God, it pleases him. *Let children draw as many stars as they like.*

Abram couldn't count the stars, but he could believe that God was going to keep his promise. From Abram we can learn to trust God...no matter what.

Let's pray. ❤ Dear God, help me to trust you to keep your promises to me...no matter what. Amen. ❤

Was Sarah As Old As My Grandma When She Had Isaac?

THEME

Nothing is too hard for God.

BIBLE REFERENCE
Genesis 21:1-7; Jeremiah 32:17

SIMPLE SUPPLIES
You'll need a Bible and several pictures of people doing difficult jobs, such as a doctor, an astronaut, a soldier, or a teacher.

Let the children respond to the following questions. What's something you think would be difficult to do? What makes a job easy? What makes a job hard? Some people can do very difficult jobs, such as take a rocket far into space or build tall skyscrapers or help a person who is sick to feel better.

Hand out the pictures of people doing difficult jobs, and let the children briefly share their responses. Look at these pictures and tell me why some of these jobs might be difficult to do.

Some things are easy to do, others are hard, and sometimes a job is absolutely impossible for anyone to do. That's never true of God though. Can you think of anything that is too hard for God to do? *Let children respond.*

The Bible tells us what God is able to do. *Read Jeremiah 32:17.* What are some things that only God can do? Why can't people do these things? *Let children respond.*

Abraham and his wife, Sarah, had been waiting and waiting for something only God could do. They were waiting for a baby. God had promised to give them a son. They waited five years. They waited ten years. More than twenty years passed and still there was no baby. Abraham and Sarah were very old.

What do we know about God when he makes a promise? We know that he keeps every promise he ever made. We also know that nothing is too hard for our great God.

Open your Bible to Genesis 21:1-3. In Genesis 21:1-3 the Bible tells us what God did for Abraham and Sarah. *Read the passage.*

How old do you think Abraham and Sarah were when they had Isaac? In Genesis 21:5 God tells us that Abraham was one hundred years old! We know from other verses in the Bible that Sarah was over ninety years old! When Isaac was born, Abraham and Sarah were probably older than your grandparents. That seems impossible to us, but God showed that nothing is too hard for him to do.

What are some things that are hard for you to do? What are things that seem impossible for you to do? *Let the children respond.* Maybe it's hard for you to be kind to those who are unkind. Maybe it's difficult for you to be patient or let others go first. When we ask God to help us, we should remember that we have a powerful God, and even when things are hard for us, nothing is too hard for God.

Let's pray together. ❤ Dear God, help us remember that nothing is ever too hard for you. Thank you for being our great and mighty God who is able to do all that you have promised to do. Amen. ❤

Why Was Esau So Hairy?

THEME

God makes us special.

BIBLE REFERENCE

Genesis 27:1-40

SIMPLE SUPPLIES

You'll need a Bible, a pair of sunglasses, an adult dress shirt, a hat, and a necktie, and one star-shaped sticker or paper star for each child.

I am going to pick a volunteer to help me with our Bible story today. *Choose a child to stand in front of the other children.* This is [child's name]. I want all of you except [child's name] to close your eyes until I tell you to open them. *While the children's eyes are closed, place the dress shirt, sunglasses, tie, and hat on your volunteer. Ask the children to open their eyes.* Who do I have here? *Allow children to answer.* But this doesn't look like [child's name]. [Child's name] wouldn't wear these clothes. *Direct this question to the child.* Who are you? How do you know who you are?

Ask the other children the following questions. Why didn't this disguise fool you? How did you know who this was? If I dressed differently, would that make me a different person? Do you think how we change on the outside changes who we are on the inside?

Take the clothes back off the child and allow him or her to sit with the group. Today's Bible story is about two brothers named Esau and Jacob. Jacob actually did wear a disguise and fooled his father into thinking he was his brother, Esau. Listen as I read some verses from Genesis 27 in my Bible. *Read Genesis 27:1-2,15-24 to the children.*

Esau had a lot of hair and Jacob didn't. To steal a special blessing from Esau, Jacob dressed up and pretended to be Esau. He wore his brother's clothes and even goatskins to fool his father. Jacob thought if he looked like Esau, he could be like Esau and have what Esau had. Jacob didn't think about what made *him* special, he tried to be someone else to be special.

Let children respond to these questions. Who are some people you try to dress like or act like? Why do you want to be like them? Did you ever fool anyone into thinking you were someone else? Why can't we ever wear a disguise to fool God?

Although some people can be fooled into thinking we are someone different, God knows who we are, no matter what we wear or how we act, because he made us. God loves us for who we are, on the inside and the outside, even when we don't love certain things about ourselves. He wants us to know that we're special. We don't know why God makes us all so different, but we do know that God makes us special. Esau was hairy because God made him that way. You are the way you are because God made you special.

I am going to recite a poem to help you remember that you are special. *Say the following poem.*

Star light, star bright,

God made *me* a star all right!

Every day

And every night,

I'm always special in God's sight.

Let's repeat the poem together to remind us of who we are. *Have the children recite each line after you so that they can memorize this poem together. After you have taught the poem, hand each child a star.* You may put your name or draw your face on the star when you get home. This star shows that you're an "all-star" and don't need to be like someone else to be special.

Let's pray. ❤ Dear Lord, thank you for making each one of us special. Help us to remember that you made us to be different from each other and to be special in your eyes. Amen. ❤

Why Didn't Joseph Just Share His Coat?

THEME

God loves everyone equally.

BIBLE REFERENCE

Genesis 37:1-4

SIMPLE SUPPLIES

You'll need a Bible and a bag with one small treat (such as a sticker, candy, or party favor) for each child.

Demonstrate *the following movements as you speak.* Please stand and move so that you can hold your arms straight out on each side of your body, palms up. You're going to pretend to be a scale that weighs fair and unfair things. When I say something that's unfair, I want you to lower your left hand and raise your right hand up a little. When I say something that someone does to make things fair, l want you to lower your right hand and bring your left hand up a little. *Practice being a scale with the children by giving them these examples: You got yelled at for something that wasn't your fault (lower left arm, raise right); your friend found ten dollars, then turned it in so that the owner could get it back (lower right arm, raise left). Younger children may need help in telling right from left.*

Now I'm going to tell you a story from the Bible, and we'll use our scales to see what was fair and unfair. Let's begin with our scales in the balanced position.

Jacob had twelve sons who all did chores. That's pretty fair. Let's keep our arms balanced. Jacob loved one son, Joseph, more than the other sons. *Let them lower left arms.* Jacob gave Joseph a special coat and didn't give the other sons anything. *Let them lower left arms farther.* This coat was special, and made it clear that Jacob loved Joseph much more than he loved his other sons. That must have really hurt their feelings! Not fair! *Drop the left arm lower.* Jacob didn't see why the other sons were upset. *Let children put left arms as low as possible with the right arms very high.*

Tell me what Jacob could have done to be fair. *After the children give a few examples, let them raise the left arm and bring down the right arm a little.* What could Joseph's brothers have said or done to make things fair? *Let the children lower the right arm a little after they give examples.* If you were Joseph, what would you have done? *Have the children give some ideas and then put their arms back to a "balanced scale" position, arms straight out like at the beginning. Ask children to put their arms down and sit.*

This is the story from Genesis 37:1-4. *Read the verses.* Do you think God liked what Jacob did? Why did Jacob give only Joseph a special coat? How do you think Joseph felt? *Allow children to respond.*

Joseph probably felt good to feel his father's love. He must have been proud to wear such a special coat. Since almost all his brothers were older, he didn't have to share, because the coat wouldn't fit them. Joseph could have shared his coat, but even sharing his coat wouldn't have made his father love the other brothers as much as he loved Joseph. And it's likely that Joseph didn't share because he liked the attention, even though it made his brothers angry. Have you had times when someone treated you better than everyone else? How did you feel? What did you do? *Let children respond.*

A lot of times we feel more like Joseph's brothers than Joseph. How do you think Joseph's brothers felt? *Let children respond.*

Sometimes our lives seem unfair. We wish we could have special gifts and attention. But we can't always balance the scales. We can't always make things fair. Sometimes people will treat us like Joseph, but sometimes we'll feel like Joseph's brothers when we're treated unfairly.

The good news is that God is always fair. God doesn't choose to love some people more than others. God loves everyone equally. While we can't make people love each other the same, we do know that God loves each of us the same amount.

Let's thank God for loving us equally. ♥ Dear God, thank you that you don't love one of us more than the others. Thank you that you love each one of us equally. Help us to treat each other the way you treat us. Amen. ♥

Hold up your bag of treats. If I gave this bag of treats to one person, it would be unfair. God wants us to love each other the same and treat each other fairly as he does. Take this treat, and remember that God loves everyone equally. *Hand out treats to all of the children.*

Do My Dreams Tell the Future Like Joseph's Dreams Did?

THEME

God is in charge of the future.

BIBLE REFERENCE
Genesis 37:5-10; 41:25-32

SIMPLE SUPPLIES
You'll need a Bible, two hard-boiled eggs, one half-full clear glass of water, and one half-full clear glass of water with as much salt as possible stirred into it *and completely dissolved* (at least three tablespoons of salt).

How many of you are good at guessing games? Why is it so much fun to guess what's going to happen next? What do you think will happen tomorrow? Can we know what the future will be like? *Let the children respond.*

Let's play a guessing game. We're going to put each of these eggs in a different glass of water. What do you think is going to happen to the eggs? Why? *Allow children to respond.*

Allow a child to slowly drop the first egg into the first glass filled with plain water. Was your guess correct? *Allow children to respond.*

Pick another child to carefully drop the second egg into the other glass. If you've used enough salt, the egg in the salt water will float. The egg in plain water will sink to the bottom. Did you expect both eggs to do the same thing? Why don't we like it when our guesses aren't right? Why do we want to know what will happen in the future? *Allow children to respond.*

Open your Bible to Genesis 37. Joseph was a man in the Bible. With God's help, Joseph could tell what was going to happen in the future. The Bible says that God gave Joseph dreams to show him what was going to happen both to him and to other people. *Read Genesis 37:5-10 aloud.* This is one example of Joseph telling what would happen in the future through his understanding of dreams. What Joseph said made his family very angry, but later everything he said did come true. God helped Joseph understand that he should use his gift to help other people.

Some people wish they could be like Joseph and have dreams telling what will happen in the future. But if we know the future, we don't have to trust in God, and God wants us to trust him rather than trust what people predict about the future. God is in charge of the future. God loves us and doesn't want us to worry about things that are going to happen on another day.

Why do you think people worry so much about the future? What can we do to keep from worrying about what will happen tomorrow? Why is it important for each of us to trust God? *Let the children discuss the questions.*

Let's pray to God. ❤ God, we thank you for being in charge of the future. We are glad that we can trust you to take care of us today, tomorrow, and for all the days to come. Amen. ❤

Why Did Pharaoh Keep Changing His Mind About Letting the Israelites Go?

THEME

God keeps his word.

BIBLE REFERENCE

Exodus 5–12

SIMPLE SUPPLIES

You'll need a Bible, dry-erase board, ruler, marker, and eraser. Before the lesson, use the ruler to draw two horizontal lines parallel to each other, *exactly* the same length. Following the example below, on the top line, add v-shaped arrows on each end of the line so that each v points into and touches the end of that line.
On the bottom line, add v-shaped arrows so that each end has an arrow pointing out away from the line that it is touching.

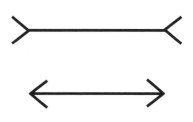

Show the children the dry-erase board with the different arrows. Ask them to tell you which line is longer. Use the ruler to measure the lines and show them that they are equal in length even though they don't look the same. This is an optical illusion. Our eyes fooled us into believing something that wasn't true. The Bible tells us about a man called Pharaoh who was a little like this optical illusion. He kept fooling the people of Israel and made them believe he would keep his promises.

Sometimes people are not always as they appear. They can be like optical illusions, fooling us into believing something that's not true. People can make and break promises to us.

Open your Bible to Exodus 6. The Bible, in the book of Exodus, tells how God sent plagues, or serious troubles, to force Pharaoh to free the Israelites who he was using as slaves. Every time there was a plague, Pharaoh promised that if God would make the plague go away he would let the Israelites go free. But every time the plague was gone, Pharaoh went back on his promise and forced the Israelites to do even harder work. Why do you think he did that? Why didn't he have to keep his promises? *Allow children to respond.*

The Bible also tells us in Exodus that God promised he would free the Israelites. Even though Pharaoh kept breaking his promise, God did make a way for the Israelites to escape from Pharaoh. Did God have to keep his promises? Why do you think God kept his word? *Allow children to respond.*

God always keeps his word. He doesn't break his promises. Even though people may lie, God never lies. He always tells us the truth. *Use the eraser to remove the arrows from each line.* God is not like an optical illusion, God is like an equal sign. God equals truth. God will never fool us or lie to us.

What are some promises God has given us? For example, we know he promised that Jesus would come again someday. *Let the children answer.*

We can read about God's promises in the Bible and see that God keeps his word. Many things God has promised have already come true. Remember, God is great, God is true, God always keeps his word to you. *Have the children repeat this phrase with you.*

Let's have everyone stand as we join together in prayer. *Have the children stand and face you.* ❤ Dear God, thank you for keeping your word. Thank you for the promises you give us. We are glad that we have the Bible and can see how you have always kept your promises. Help us to be more like you and keep our promises too. Amen. ❤

Why Did God Send All Those Plagues on Egypt?

THEME

God takes care of us.

BIBLE REFERENCE

Exodus 5–12; Romans 8:38-39

SIMPLE SUPPLIES

You'll need a Bible, a permanent marker, and two inflated round balloons. Before children arrive, use the marker to write "God" on one balloon and "Me" on the other, with the words right side up as the balloons are hung from the tied ends.

oday we're going to learn about the ten plagues that God sent the Egyptians. The Egyptians wouldn't let the people of Israel, who were God's special people, leave Egypt, because they had made the Israelites into slaves. Slaves had to work very hard and could not do what they wanted. God had promised that he would free the Israelites so that they wouldn't be slaves anymore and could live in their own land instead of Egypt. Even though life was hard for the Israelites while they were slaves, God was taking care of them.

God sent Moses to tell Pharaoh, the king of Egypt, to let the Israelites go free. *Read Exodus 5:1-2.* Pharaoh didn't want the Israelites to be free. He didn't want them to leave Egypt or worship God. He didn't want to listen to God, so God sent plagues, or troubles, to let Pharaoh know that God was in charge and should be obeyed.

Listen to this poem about the ten plagues God sent.

Blood, frogs, gnats, and flies,

God had heard Israel's cries.

Livestock died, sores, and hail,

God's promise would prevail.

Locusts, darkness, the night of Passover,

Israel was free and moving over.

God took care of the people of Israel just as he had promised. God used the plagues to show Pharaoh that he was in charge and to make him let the Israelites go free. Through all of this, God protected the Israelites from the plagues and then God protected them and cared for them when Pharaoh finally set them free. What are some ways that God takes care of you? *Let children respond.*

Hold up the two balloons, one in each hand, making sure you hold them by the ends so that they can swing freely. Let's let one balloon represent God and the other balloon represent each of us. *Pick a child to stand beside you. Hold the balloons apart on either side of the child's mouth, about three inches apart and not touching the child's face.* Pretend there's some kind of trouble trying to keep you away from God. Blow really hard in between both balloons to show that there's something trying to keep you from God. Keep blowing until I tell you to stop. *Keep the child blowing between the balloons until the two balloons touch together.* Stop. What happened to the balloons? Why do you think they blew together instead of apart? *Allow another child to blow in between the balloons. Repeat with different children as time allows.*

Even when difficult things try to keep us away from God, God takes care of us and brings us closer to him. *Read Romans 8:38-39.* Nothing can keep God's love away from us. God takes care of us because he loves us.

💜 Lord, thank you that you take care of us even when there are troubles around us. Help us remember to trust you to care for us each day. Amen. 💜

What Did Manna Taste Like?

THEME

God gives us good things.

BIBLE REFERENCE

Exodus 16:1-31

SIMPLE SUPPLIES

You'll need a Bible, a large glass almost full of water, a towel, a bag of marbles, angel food cake pieces on a plate, and honey in a bowl.

et the glass of water on the towel. Hand several older volunteers a few marbles each.

Let's name as many good things from God as we can. Every time someone names something good that God gives us, our volunteers will put one marble into the glass. We'll see if all the marbles will go into the glass without spilling the water. What are some good things God gives us? *As the children answer, have the volunteers take turns adding one marble to the glass of water for each answer given. Stop when the water overflows.*

God gives us so many good things that the water spilled over the edge of the cup! An overflowing cup reminds us that we have so many good things in our lives that we can't even hold onto them. We can't name everything God gives us, because he gives us so much.

God gave good things to the people of Israel, too. God had made a way for them to escape being slaves, but they had to go through a huge desert where there weren't any towns. This meant there was no way for them to buy food. What would you do if you were the Israelites far away from any place to get food, with no cars, no telephones, or any other way to get food? *Let children respond.* Let's see what God did. *Read Exodus 16:14-15, 31 to the children.*

How do you think the Israelites felt when they saw and tasted the food God sent? *Let children respond.* God could have given them Brussels sprouts, lima beans, spinach, or even hot peppers. These people were so hungry, they would have been grateful for *any* kind of food. What does the Bible say manna tasted like? God gave them something good.

Let's have angel food cake dipped it in honey to get an idea of what manna might have tasted like. *Ask the children to line up, and tell them to take a piece of cake and dip it in the bowl of honey.* How does it taste? Do you think you would have liked manna? Why or why not? *Let the children answer.*

It's unlikely that we would get lost and hungry in the wilderness like the people of Israel did. But there may be sad times in our lives when we're not sure what to do. These are the times that we can ask God for help. God probably won't send manna, but he will send us what we need.

Let's pray. ❤ Lord, thank you that you give us so many good things. Help us to be thankful for the good things you provide. Amen. ❤

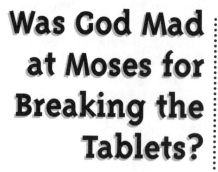

Was God Mad at Moses for Breaking the Tablets?

THEME

God gives us second chances.

BIBLE REFERENCE

Exodus 32:1-20; 34:1-10

SIMPLE SUPPLIES

You'll need a Bible, a broken pencil, a pencil sharpener, several broken toys or household items (without sharp edges), and one unsharpened pencil for each child.

Place the broken items where the children can see them. I have some items I want to show you. *Allow the children to answer the following questions.* What do these items have in common? How many of you have ever broken something? What happens after someone breaks something?

Open your Bible to Exodus 32. God had written his special laws on big slabs of stone that we call stone tablets. The Bible tells in Exodus 32 about a time when Moses broke the stone tablets—on purpose! While Moses was getting God's commandments, the people were already disobeying by worshipping a statue instead of God. Moses broke the tablets out of anger because the people of Israel were disobeying God's laws. Do you think God was angry at Moses for breaking the stone tablets? Was God angry at the people for breaking his laws? *Let children respond.* Later Moses went back to God, and God wrote the laws on new stone tablets. Why do you think God gave the people a second chance to obey him? *Let children respond.*

Hold up some of the broken objects. Can some of these objects be fixed? How would you fix them? How do we fix the rules we break? *Let the children respond.*

Some things are easier to fix than others. We can use glue or tape to fix broken objects, but it's harder to fix mistakes that we make. It's also hard to take care of the wrong things or sins that we do.

Display a broken pencil. This pencil point can be fixed with a pencil sharpener. *Sharpen the pencil.* When we sharpen a pencil, we take off the broken part and make a new point so that the pencil can be useful once more. We're like broken pencils, breaking God's laws instead of doing right. God is like a sharpener, taking away our brokenness and making us like new again.

God gives second chances. God didn't glue together the stone tablets that Moses broke; he made new ones, as a new start for everyone. God was angry, but he loved the people enough to give them another chance.

I'm going to give you each a new pencil to keep. When you write with it, I'd like you to think of how God has written his laws for you in the Bible. When you break the point or need to sharpen this pencil, remember that when we're sorry, God gives us a second chance. *Hand out the pencils.*

Let's join together in a prayer. ❤ Heavenly Father, thank you for giving us second chances. We're sorry that we sin and break your laws. We ask that you forgive us. Amen. ❤

Why Did the Israelites March Around the Wall of Jericho Seven Times?

THEME
God teaches us patience.

BIBLE REFERENCE
Joshua 6:1-20

SIMPLE SUPPLIES
You'll need a Bible, a watch, and an instant-print camera with film.

Take an instant-print picture of the group, and place it in the middle of the floor. Let's stand and march around the picture. We have to keep marching until the picture develops. *Check the time on your watch. Help everyone march slowly around the picture.*

Is it ready yet? No? Let's keep marching. How about now? Still not ready? We've got to keep going. Keep marching! It's hard to wait, isn't it? Does it help time go faster if we're marching? *Keep marching until the picture is fully developed. Note how long it took the picture to develop.*

Allow the children to sit down and pass the picture around as they respond to these questions. How long did it seem like we were marching? *Give the correctly timed answer after they guess.* Were you glad you had something to do? What are some things we have to wait for? Where are places we have to wait a lot? *Allow children to respond to each question.*

In the book of Joshua, the people of Israel had to wait a long time for one of God's promises to come true. Not only that, but they had to do several things first before God would fulfill his promise. Joshua 6 tell us about the walls of Jericho falling down after the Israelites marched around and around and around the city. For six days they marched once around the city of Jericho, and then on the seventh day, they marched *seven* times around the city. Here's what the Bible says. *Read Joshua 6:15-16, 20 to the children.*

How would you like to march for six days? How would you feel about marching around a city seven times on the seventh day after marching so much before that day? *Allow students to answer.*

God made sure the people were willing to obey him by giving them a task to do. God taught them to be patient by waiting for God's promises. He wanted them to learn that he was in charge and that patience is rewarded.

God teaches us patience too. He answers our prayers in his time and in his way. He asks us to trust him and obey him. We need to follow God's plans just like the Israelites.

Hold up the picture of the group. It's hard to wait. We're not patient people. God teaches us patience. We can practice being patient people by doing his work while waiting for God's promises to come true.

❤ Dear God, Thank you for keeping your promises to us. Please give us patience and let us trust and obey you always. Amen. ❤

Did Samson Eat Spinach?

THEME

God gives us strength to do his work.

BIBLE REFERENCE
Judges 16

SIMPLE SUPPLIES
You'll need a Bible, a straight-back chair with no armrests, a sports drink bottle, a wrapped protein bar, and a small weight.

How strong are you? What do you do to become stronger? *Allow the children to respond.* I have some things that might help. *Pass around the sports drink bottle, wrapped protein bar, and small weight.* Do these things make us stronger? How? *Allow children to respond, then collect the items and put them away.*

We use many different things to become stronger. What could you do if you were stronger? *Have the children respond.* Let's flex our arm muscles to see how strong they are. We can try an experiment to see how strong we are too.

Place a chair in the middle of the group. Have a child sit in the chair with his or her back against the chair back, feet firmly on the floor, arms folded, head back, and chin up. Choose another child to come forward and press just his or her index finger against the seated child's forehead making sure to keep the child's head toward the back of the chair. Ask the child in the chair to stand while keeping his or her arms folded. The child in the chair will be unable to stand. Let other children try this as time allows. This works best with children who are about the same size.

This works for us, no matter how strong we are, because the person who is sitting is unable to shift his or her center of gravity which is needed to stand up. That's a great little trick to make us look strong. The Bible tells about a man who didn't need any tricks to be strong. His name was Samson. Have you ever heard of him? The Bible says Samson was so strong he could fight wild animals and defend himself from at least a thousand attackers. How do you think he got his strength? *Let children share their answers.*

The Bible tells us in the book of Judges that Samson obeyed special guidelines from God such as not cutting his hair. These things didn't make him strong though, they just showed that Samson was obeying God. God was the one who gave Samson his strength. While it's important to eat right and exercise to build our muscles, we have to remember that God gives us strength to do his work.

Let children respond to these questions. What are some things we can do right now for God? What are things we can do right, no matter how strong or weak we are? What can we do to become stronger Christians? What kind of *spiritual* food and exercise do we need to follow God?

Open your Bible to Judges 16, and show it to the children. The Bible tells us in Judges 16 how Samson began to make bad choices. Samson didn't always remember that his strength came from God. When Samson disobeyed God, his strength was taken away from him.

We have to remember that our strength comes from God and should be used for God's work. Even when we're children, we can be strong enough to do God's work. We are strong because God makes us strong.

❤ Dear God, thank you for giving us strength to do what you want us to do. Please help us to obey you and use our strength to do what's right. Amen. ❤

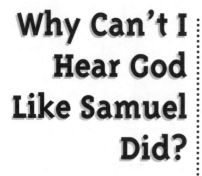

Why Can't I Hear God Like Samuel Did?

THEME

God talks to us and calls us.

BIBLE REFERENCE
1 Samuel 3:1-11

SIMPLE SUPPLIES
You'll need a Bible and two working cell phones.

Arrange for someone (who the children can't see) to call you on your cell phone the first time you say Samuel's name. I'm glad you could be here today because I have an important story to tell you. My Bible story is about a boy named Samuel. When Samuel was a boy, he lived in the Temple with a priest named Eli. *Stop talking when the phone rings.* Hold on a minute, I have a call. *Answer phone.* Hello? Hello? I must have just missed it, there's no one there. What do you think I should do now? *Allow the children to answer.*

That might have been an important call since it interrupted us. How do I find out who called me? What are some ways you find out who's called you on the phone? *Let children answer.* I guess I'll have to wait for that person to call me back.

In the meantime, I was telling you about Samuel, a young boy who lived a long time ago. Samuel received a call too, but his call was from God. *Read 1 Samuel 3:1-11, then let the children answer the following questions.* What would you have done if you were Samuel? Why do you think Samuel didn't know that God was talking to him? How did Eli know it was God?

God was patient with Samuel. He had to call him three times before Samuel listened to him. God is patient with us, too, because sometimes we don't recognize our call from God. God can interrupt our lives at unexpected times and speak to us anywhere.

How do you speak to God? *Hold your hand to the side of your face with your thumb pointing at your ear, the top three fingers curled and the pinkie extended toward your mouth like a phone.* I want you to put your hand up to your ear and pretend to talk out loud to God. *Give children a moment to talk.* Now let's stop talking aloud, because God can hear us even if we talk to him in our hearts. *Hold up your cell phone.* When we're on the phone, we have to listen as well as talk. We can't hear God if we don't listen.

God doesn't call us on a phone, but picks different ways to talk to us. How do you think God talks to us? *Let children respond.* He talks to us through the Bible, through other people, and through our prayers.

I'd like you to hold up a fist, then close your eyes. Let's stop talking and be very still and quiet. When I tell you to listen, try to hear three different sounds. Every time you hear a different sound, I want you to put up one finger. When you've heard three different sounds and have uncurled three fingers on your hand, you may open your eyes, but you must stay quiet and still until everyone has three fingers up. Now close your eyes and listen really, really carefully. *Allow the children time to listen, and wait until everyone has their fingers in the air.*

What are some of the different sounds you heard? Could you hear these things when we were all talking? Why was it easier to listen when you were still and quiet? *Let children respond.*

Samuel heard God when he was still and quiet. We're more likely to hear God when we're still and quiet too. We may not hear God the same way Samuel did, but we know that God wants to speak to all of us. He is calling us to do his work.

Let's pray together. ❤ Dear God, help us listen for your call whenever and wherever it comes to us. Thank you for being there to listen and to talk to us. Amen. ❤

Did Goliath Live on a Beanstalk?

THEME

God can help us with our problems, no matter how big or how small!

BIBLE REFERENCE

1 Samuel 17

SIMPLE SUPPLIES

You'll need a Bible, a small potted plant, three yardsticks, a chair, and five smooth stones for each child. Before the children arrive, scatter the stones on the floor in the discussion area.

Let's look at this plant and use our imaginations. Let's imagine that this plant is a really huge, huge beanstalk. Can you pretend that with me? Stand up, and let's pretend to climb our imaginary beanstalk. *Have the children stand and pretend to climb in place. Let the children climb for about twenty seconds, commenting about how tall the beanstalk is as the children pretend to climb.* Wow! We've reached the top of the beanstalk now. You can stop climbing and sit down again.

Do you think anyone could live on a beanstalk? There's a pretend story about a giant and a beanstalk; you've probably heard of it. But that's just a pretend story. No one could really live on a beanstalk, and giants like the one in that story don't exist. But there really are people who are really tall. About seventy years ago, there was a man named Robert Wadlow who was 8 feet 11 inches tall!

There was a man in the Bible named Goliath who was even a little taller than Robert Wadlow. Compared to everyone else, he was a real giant. *Open your Bible to 1 Samuel 17, and read verse 4 aloud.* Let's see how tall nine feet is. *Using the chair, have two children help you hold three yardsticks end to end to show how tall nine feet is.* Look how tall this is! The Bible tells us that Goliath was even taller than this! *Thank the volunteers, and have them return to their seats.*

Well, not only was Goliath a big man, but he was also a big problem! His people, the Philistines, were in a war with God's people. None of God's people wanted to fight Goliath because he was so incredibly big! They were all afraid. Only one person, a young man named David, was willing to fight Goliath, because he knew that God would help him.

David had a really big problem, didn't he? Sometimes we have problems that seem really big! Sometimes our problems seem like giants! What kinds of big problems do kids have? What are really big problems that you've heard of people having? *Allow children to respond; seek answers that would be considered "big"—such as not having a home to live in, having no money for food, a parent's lost job, the death of a loved one, a serious illness, and so on.*

David knew that God would help him fight the giant. God can help us with our big problems too. God sends friends or other family members to help us. Sometimes God uses the church to help us with our big problems. God uses doctors to help us when we're sick. Often God will solve our problems with a new job, a new house, or money from a loving person. God helps us with our big problems, just as he helped David.

God helped David fight the giant. David picked up five stones from a stream. With just one of these small stones, David won the battle with the giant. God helped David with his big, big problem! Look around you on the floor. Let's be like David and each pick up five stones. *Pause while the children collect the stones. Then have the children sit while you finish the story.*

Look at your stones. They're small, aren't they? Sometimes we have problems that seem like small problems, like a hurt finger or a broken toy. Turn to your neighbor and tell him or her about one of your small problems. *Pause for children to respond.*

Even though many of our problems seem small, they are still very important to us, and those problems are also important to God. God helps us with our small problems as well as our big problems.

Take your stones home with you to remind you that God can help us with our big problems and our small problems. I'd like for you to keep one stone at home for yourself. I'd like for you to find four people this week to share the story of David and Goliath. Give each of those people one of the stones when you share the story.

Now let's thank God for helping us. ❤ Dear God, thank you for helping us with all of our problems, no matter how big or small. Amen. ❤

Why Was King Saul So Grumpy?

THEME

Sin in our lives takes away our joy.

BIBLE REFERENCE
1 Samuel 20

SIMPLE SUPPLIES
You'll need a Bible, one heart cut from red construction paper for each child, markers, and newspapers.

What makes you feel happy or joyful? What things take away that feeling of joy? How can you tell if someone has a grumpy heart or a joyful heart? *Let children respond to each question.*

Give each child a red heart, and place the markers where children can share them. As we think about joyful hearts, I'd like each of you to draw a smiley face on your heart. *Allow time for children to do this.*

Hold up your joyful hearts so we all can see them. Now place the hearts on the floor in front of you, and listen to me. God wants us to have joy in our hearts. Knowing God and having Jesus in charge of our lives gives us joy. But there's something that can hide that joy, or cover it up. What do you think that is? What makes our hearts stop having joy? *Let children share their answers.*

When we do bad things, or sin, our joy is taken away, or hidden, by that sin. Sin causes us to be unhappy and separates us from God. We can learn more about this from a man in the Bible named Saul.

In the Bible, in the book of 1 Samuel, we learn about King Saul and his son, Jonathan. *Open your Bible to 1 Samuel 20.* King Saul wanted his son, Jonathan, to be the next king. But God wanted David to be king. And on top of this, David and Jonathan were best friends. All of this made King Saul angry. In fact, he was so angry and so jealous of David that he wanted to kill David! Jonathan tried to reason with his father. Let's read what happened. *Read 1 Samuel 20:32-33.* King Saul's heart was filled with such sin that he became a very grumpy man. Sin took over King Saul's heart and took away his joy.

Sometimes we do bad things or have sin in our lives. *Hand each child a piece of the newspaper.* I'd like you to use this newspaper to represent sin. Tear off a piece of the paper. Let's pretend that paper stands for a time that you didn't obey. Lay the newspaper strip on top of your heart. Now tear another piece. We'll let that stand for a time when you said something mean to someone. Lay that paper over your heart too. Keep tearing newspaper and thinking about sins, or bad things, that you've done. When your heart is completely covered, look up at me so that I'll know you're done. *Allow time for children to work.*

What happened to our hearts? How did the sins we were thinking of cover up the joy? Sin in our lives can take away our joyful hearts. Sin can make us grumpy, just as it did to King Saul.

We can ask God to forgive us of our sins. When we ask him to take away our sin, we can have joyful hearts again. Let's ask God to take away our sins.

❤ Dear God, please forgive us of the wrong things that we do. Please help us not to sin. Take away our sin so that we may have joyful hearts. Thank you for your forgiveness. Amen. ❤

Because God forgives our sins, let's remove the newspaper strips. When we remove the "sin," what's left? You're right—a joyful heart!

Why Didn't David Get Even With Saul When He Had the Chance?

THEME

God wants us to do what's right.

BIBLE REFERENCE

1 Samuel 24

SIMPLE SUPPLIES

You'll need a Bible and a small piece of cloth with a ragged edge.

It's not always easy to do the right thing. How do you know right from wrong? How do you decide whether you're going to do right or wrong? What happens when you do what's wrong even though you know the right thing to do? *Allow children to respond to each question.*

Open your Bible to 1 Samuel 24. The Bible tells us in 1 Samuel 24 about King Saul and how he was chasing after David and trying to kill him. King Saul knew that God wanted David to be the next king. This made King Saul very angry. He was so angry that he wanted to get rid of David.

David followed God and wanted to do what was right, even though he had to run away and hide to keep from being killed. At one point, David and the men who traveled with him hid in a cave. Let's pretend we're with David and his men and huddle very close together. *Squeeze everyone close together as if you're hiding. Begin talking softly, but so that children can hear you.* We'll have to whisper very quietly so no one will know we're in here!

David hid from King Saul in a cave. What do you think it might have been like in the cave? *Let children answer.* While King Saul was looking for David, King Saul went into the very same cave where David was hiding! Now we really have to be quiet! King Saul didn't know David was in the cave, but David and his men knew that King Saul was in the cave. Let's read what the men and David did. *Read 1 Samuel 24:4 aloud.* David sneaked up on King Saul and used his sword to cut off a small piece of King Saul's robe. *Hold up the cloth.* Even though he hadn't hurt Saul, David later felt bad for even cutting Saul's robe. After King Saul left the cave and had gone some distance away, David called to him and showed him the piece of cloth. King Saul knew that David could have killed him while he was in the cave, but David spared his life. David knew it would be wrong to kill the king, even though the king was trying to kill David. David wanted to do what was right.

God wants us to do what's right too. God always wants us to choose right from wrong. Let's practice choosing what's right.

Let's start by imagining a brother and sister are playing. The brother grabs a toy from his sister's hand because he wants to play with that toy. His sister begins to cry. If you were the brother, what would be the right thing to do? If you were the sister, what would be the right thing to do? *Let children share their answers.*

That was great! Let's try another one. Let's pretend that your mom asked you to clean your room before you have a snack. You start to clean your room, but decide you're really hungry. Mom is busy and isn't in the kitchen. You really want a snack now. What should you do? What is the right thing to do? *Let children share their answers.*

Let's pretend you're watching television. A show that you are allowed to watch has just finished. Another program is coming on that your dad doesn't allow you to watch. You know that your dad isn't paying attention and won't know what you're watching. What's the right thing to do? *Let children share their answers.*

David had the chance to kill King Saul and keep King Saul from chasing him. But David wanted to do what was right. David cut off a small part of King Saul's robe, but did not harm King Saul. God wants us to do what's right too. Even when it's hard, let's remember David and choose to do what's right.

Let's pray. ❤ Dear God, please help us always to choose what is right. Thank you for showing us right from wrong. Amen. ❤

Was Solomon Smarter Than Jesus?

THEME

Real wisdom requires faith.

BIBLE REFERENCE

1 Kings 3:1-15

SIMPLE SUPPLIES

You'll need a plastic food container, a large bowl of rice, one plastic spoon per child, and a wooden cross that will fit inside the food container. Before the activity, use a permanent marker to draw a face on your container lid.

Raise your hand if you think you're smart. I want to see everyone's hand raised high in the air. God made each and every one of you smart. God gave us wisdom. Sometimes we may be smarter in one area than we are in another area, but you are all very smart.

Open your Bible to 1 Kings 3:1-15. The Bible tells us of a wise king named King Solomon. One night, God appeared to King Solomon in a dream. God told King Solomon that he could ask for anything he wanted. King Solomon asked for wisdom to rule God's people. King Solomon wanted to be wise. Listen to what God said to Solomon. *Read 1 Kings 3:12 aloud.*

God made it so that other than Jesus, Solomon was the wisest man who ever lived. In the book of Proverbs, Solomon often talked about how knowing and respecting God was the most important part of wisdom. You can fill your head with all sorts of things, but if you don't know God, your smarts aren't worth too much. Let me show you what I mean.

Let's pretend this container is your head, and let's say the rice is the stuff you put in your head like math, reading, and even cartoons. Let's each put some stuff in this head. *Have children each put a spoonful of rice in your container. As children put in the rice, have them each say one thing we put in our heads such as TV shows or school subjects.*

Have children continue to add rice until the container is pouring over. Then pull out your cross. Now that we've put all this stuff in here, there's no room for the most important thing of all—faith. Without faith, we can't have real wisdom—we just have a lot of facts and information. Let's start over.

Dump out the rice, and repeat the exercise. This time put the cross into the container before pouring in the rice. It's good to learn as much as we can about the world God made and the people in it. But we need to remember to put Jesus first in our lives. When he is most important, the things we learn become real wisdom. Jesus is the beginning of all real wisdom.

♥ Dear God, thank you for the wisdom that you give us. Help us to use that wisdom to choose right from wrong. Help us to use our wisdom to learn more about you. Amen. ♥

Did the Ravens Bring Toys and Games to Elijah Too?

THEME

God takes care of our needs.

BIBLE REFERENCE

1 Kings 17:1-6

SIMPLE SUPPLIES

You'll need a Bible, one craft feather for each child, a sign that says "Want," a sign that says "Need," and small crackers or bits of bread. Have an adult male volunteer sit at the front away from the group. This volunteer will be Elijah. Place a blue sheet or towel on the floor next to him as a brook.

We're going to play a game called "Need It or Want It." *Have one child stand on each side of you. Give one the "Need" sign and the other the "Want" sign.* I'm going to name some things, and you're going to decide if this is something that you need in order to live or if it's something that you want to have. Show if you think what I say is a need or want by pointing to one of these signs.

Let's start with water. Show if this is a want or a need by the way you point. *Allow children to point, then let them put their hands down and answer these questions.* Does your body need water to live? What happens if we don't get enough water? You're right. This is a need and not just a want.

The next word is "computer." *Let kids point to indicate their answers, then share their answers.* Do we need computers in order to live? When are computers helpful? Even if they're helpful, do we need them to live? I guess this is a want.

Continue playing, naming food, video games, shoes, dolls or action figures, shelter, and other items as time allows. Some items may not clearly be wants or needs. For example, we don't need shoes to survive, but we need them to protect our feet so we can go to school and play outdoors. Let children share their thoughts on the different items and why they think the items are wants or needs. Then have your volunteers sit down.

You all did a great job with our game! The Bible tells us that God will take care of our needs. God often blesses us with things that we don't need but want to have, like toys, games, special clothes, and vacations. We can be very thankful that God blesses us with more than we need. Sometimes God meets our needs in unusual ways, like he did with a man in the Bible.

God took care of the needs of a man named Elijah. *Open your Bible to*

1 Kings 17:1-6. Elijah was God's prophet, which means he told people the things that God wanted them to know. One time there were people angry at Elijah because of what God told him to say. God was showing and telling the people how wrong they were acting by serving other gods. God made a time without rain—which meant there wasn't enough food and water to go around.

God took care of Elijah by telling him where to go to hide from the angry people. *Point to your adult volunteer.* We have someone pretending to be Elijah right over there. He must be in hiding beside that brook of water. Listen to what else God did. *Read 1 Kings 17:4-6 aloud.* Birds sent by God fed Elijah! Let's pretend we're birds taking bread to Elijah. *Give each child a feather and a bit of bread. Have the children "fly" over to Elijah and drop the bread on his lap, then fly back to their seats. Encourage your volunteer to play the part of Elijah as the bread is dropped.*

Can you imagine being fed by birds each day? And drinking all your water from a brook? What do you think that was like? Do you think God let the ravens bring toys and games to Elijah? Why or why not? *Pause for the children to respond to each question.*

Elijah didn't need toys and games to survive, although they might have been fun to play with. The Bible tells us that the ravens brought food and meat and Elijah had water from the brook. God took care of Elijah's needs.

Let's thank God for taking care of our needs and for blessing us with things we don't need.

💜 Dear God, thank you for taking care of our needs. Thank you for food to eat, water to drink, clothes to wear, a place to live, and the love of family and friends. We thank you, too, for the extra things you bless us with, like toys, games, televisions, cars, and other nice blessings. Amen. 💜

Was Esther Prettier Than Snow White?

THEME

God looks at our hearts.

BIBLE REFERENCE

1 Samuel 16:7c; Esther 2

SIMPLE SUPPLIES

You'll need a Bible, one hand-held mirror for every four or five children, one heart cut from red construction paper, two crowns cut from construction paper, and masking tape.

Hold up a mirror and gaze into it. Mirror, mirror in my hand, who's the most beautiful (or handsome) teacher in all the land? *Pause and look at the children.* Does that remind anyone of a fairy tale? What story does that remind you of? *Pause for an answer.* You're right! That sounds a little like what happened in the fairy tale called "Snow White." Who can tell me about Snow White? Did that story really happen? Was Snow White a real person? *Pause and let children respond.*

You're right! That story was just pretend. Snow White was not a real person. I want to tell you about a real beautiful woman who was a real person. Her name was Esther, and we can read about her in the Bible in the book of Esther. *Open your Bible to Esther 2, and show it to the children.* I'm going to let several of you help me act out this story.

In the book of Esther, we read about King Xerxes *(give a boy a paper crown to wear)* and Queen Vashti. Xerxes decided he wanted a new queen, so he took the crown from Queen Vashti and looked around for someone else to be queen. *Give the king a crown.*

King Xerxes chose a new queen, a woman named Esther. *Have the king give the crown to a girl to wear.* Esther was a very beautiful young woman. But do you know what was more important than how beautiful Esther was on the outside? Esther was beautiful on the inside, too! Esther had a beautiful heart! *Tape a construction paper heart on "Esther."* Her inside beauty came be-cause she loved the Lord. Since she loved God, God used Esther to save the Jews from being killed. God knew what was in Esther's heart. She was beautiful on the outside and, more important, she was beautiful on the inside.

God looks at our hearts too. God looks inside us to see what kind of people we are. 1 Samuel 16:7 says, "Man looks at the outward appearance, but the Lord looks at the heart." God doesn't think our looks on the outside are very important. What's important to God is the kind of people we are on the inside.

Let's use our mirrors to look at the outside of our bodies. *Have children form small groups, and give each group a mirror to share.* Take turns holding the mirror in front of your face and telling the friends in your group about what you see. You can tell your friends about the color of your eyes and hair, the shape of your face, and if you have freckles or not. *Allow a few minutes for this.* After you've told your friends about what you look like on the outside, tell them a little about what you look like on the inside. Tell your friends if you are kind to others, if you share, if you love God, if you're a good helper. Share with your friends what they would see if they could look at your heart. *Allow time for sharing.*

If you are doing this while adults are nearby, encourage the congregation to share the same answers with those near them.

Thank you for sharing with your friends about your outside appearances as well as your inside appearances. Remember that God thinks our "insides" are more important than our "outsides"! Think about that the next time that you look at yourself in the mirror.

❤ Dear God, thank you for making each of us just the way we are! Help us to remember that the kind of people we are on the inside is more important than how we look on the outside. Help us, also, to see the hearts of others and not just notice their outward appearance. Amen. ❤

Were Shadrach, Meshach, and Abednego Superheroes?

THEME
God can do amazing things!

BIBLE REFERENCE
Daniel 3

SIMPLE SUPPLIES
You'll need a Bible, construction paper, markers, and masking tape. Before children arrive, use the supplies to make three superhero shields. Draw a large S on a diamond-shaped piece of construction paper for each shield.

Welcome! You are just in time to see the new drama called The Superheroes. Each one of our superheroes will wear a superhero shield, like this. *Hold up one of the construction paper shields.*

First, I'd like you to meet Super Shad—that's short for Shadrach. We'll need one helper to play the part of Super Shad. *Choose one child to stand at the front, and tape a shield to this child's chest or have the volunteer hold the shield.* Super Shad, show us your muscles. Next, I'd like for you to meet Super Shac—that's short for Meshach. *Choose a child to play this part, and tape a shield on the child's chest or have the volunteer hold the shield.* Super Shac, show us how you fly in the air. Last, but not least, I'd like you to meet Super Abe—that's short for Abednego. *Choose a child to play this part, and tape a shield on the child's chest or have the volunteer hold the shield.* Super Abe, show us how brave you are by making your face of fearlessness.

The rest of you will be the supporting actors and actresses. You just follow along with what I tell you to do. Our story comes from the Bible, in Daniel chapter 3. *Open your Bible to Daniel 3.* There was once a king named Nebuchadnezzar. What a long name! Can you say that? Nebuchadnezzar. Put your hands on top of your head like a crown to act like a king, and do this every time we mention the king or say his name. Well, Nebuchadnezzar *(crowns)* built a huge statue of gold. What do you think the people did when they saw it? *Gasp, open your eyes really wide, and place your hand over your mouth as if showing astonishment. Encourage the children to do the same each time you mention the statue.*

The king *(crowns)* wanted all of the people to worship his golden statue *(astonished looks)*. The king *(crowns)* told the people that if they did not worship his golden statue *(astonished looks)*, he would throw them into a fire. *Pretend to wipe sweat off your forehead and fan yourself. Have the children do the same when you mention fire.*

Well, our superheroes—*point to the volunteers, and have them flex their muscles*—wait a minute! *Look at your Bible closely and scratch your head.* The Bible doesn't say these guys are superheroes! They were just ordinary men who loved God. And because they loved God, they didn't want to worship the king's *(crowns)* golden statue *(astonished looks)*. We'd better take off their superhero shields since these are just regular guys like you and me. *Have volunteers take off paper shields but remain standing to act out the rest of the story.*

The refusal of Shadrach, Meshach, and Abednego to bow down to this statue *(astonished looks)* made the king *(crowns)* very, very angry. *Make an angry face and encourage the children to make angry faces.* The king *(crowns)* said, "Throw them in the fire!" *(Wipe away sweat.)* Here's where the story gets amazing! God is so amazing that he kept the three men from burning in the fire *(wipe away sweat)*. God's power was wrapped around the three men, just like superhero capes. God did an amazing thing in that fiery furnace. When the king *(crowns)* and his men looked into the fire *(wipe away sweat)*, they saw four men walking, not just three. God sent an angel to protect Shadrach, Meshach, and Abednego. The three men did not burn up in the fire! *(Wipe away sweat.)*

Let's give our actors and actresses a hand! *Clap, and have volunteers sit down.*

We all know that there's no such thing as a superhero. When something amazing happened to someone in the Bible, it's because God, with his amazing power, caused that something special to happen. What are amazing things God can do in our lives? What's something amazing you've heard of God doing either for you or for someone else? *Let children answer.*

Let's pray. ❤ Dear God, thank you for doing such amazing things during Bible times, and thank you that you still do amazing things in our lives. Amen. ❤

Did Daniel Get to Pet the Lions?

THEME

God protects us.

BIBLE REFERENCE
Daniel 6

SIMPLE SUPPLIES
You'll need a Bible, crayons, and one lunch-sized paper bag for each child.

What frightens you? What are you afraid of? *Give the children time to respond.* A big, ferocious dog can be scary! Or a storm, with loud thunder and lightning. And what about snakes and spiders? There are a lot of things that can be scary. *Share one of your own fears.*

God knows all about our fears. God knows the things that frighten us, and he knows how to keep us safe. Listen to this story in the Bible about a man who needed to be protected. First, I want to give each of you a "lion." *Distribute the paper bags and put crayons where children can reach them. Let children quickly draw a face on the paper bag to make a simple puppet.* Put the paper bag on your hand so that it can be a lion puppet. Hold the bag so that you can open and close your lion's mouth.

Open your Bible to Daniel 6. This is from Daniel chapter 6. King Darius, a king who lived a long time ago, declared that everyone should pray only to him and to no one else. The king said that anyone who didn't obey would be tossed into a den of lions. Show me how you think your lions would sound if they roared loudly. *Pause.* Oh boy! That sounded really scary!

Daniel, a man who loved God, knew that this new rule by the king was wrong. Daniel knew that he should only pray to God. He continued to pray to God. When the king found out that Daniel was not obeying the king's orders, he had no choice but to throw him into the lions' den. Show me how you think your lions would sound if they were really, really hungry! *Pause.* Oh my! That is really, really scary!

The king's men put Daniel in the lions' den. Daniel may have been scared—we don't really know. But even if he was afraid of the lions, Daniel trusted God with whatever was going to happen. Show me how you think your hungry lions sounded when Daniel was first tossed into the lions' den. *Pause.* Oh my goodness! If I were Daniel, I would be afraid!

But do you know what happened? God closed the mouths of the lions! Close those mouths on your lions. Snap them shut nice and tight! Use your other hand to hold your lions' mouths closed so that they can't roar. They don't seem quite so dangerous or scary now, do they? God didn't allow the lions to eat or harm Daniel! What do you think Daniel thought about that? How do you think Daniel felt? What do you think Daniel did? Do you think Daniel petted the lions or kept his distance? *Let children respond to each question.*

We don't really know any of the answers to those questions. We can only guess the answers. Maybe Daniel thought the lions were such beautiful animals that he couldn't resist petting the lions! Or maybe he just kept to himself as far from the lions as possible. We don't know what Daniel did or how he felt. The most important part of this story is that God protected Daniel from the lions. God closed the lions' mouths.

If God can close the mouths of hungry lions, he can certainly protect us from scary things too! What are ways God can protect us? How have you felt protected during a scary time? What can you do the next time you're feeling afraid to help you remember that God protects us? *Let children respond.*

Take your lion puppets home with you. Let the lion puppet remind you that God protects you, each and every day.

❤ Dear God, thank you for protecting me. Help me to trust you so that I won't be afraid. Amen. ❤

Did Jonah Get Seasick in the Whale?

THEME

We need to obey God.

BIBLE REFERENCE

Jonah 1

SIMPLE SUPPLIES

You'll need blue paper napkins, graham crackers, bear-shaped crackers, fish-shaped crackers, and resealable sandwich bags. Make a bag for each child, containing one graham cracker square, three or four bear-shaped crackers, and several fish-shaped crackers.

Who can tell me what it means to obey? *Pause for children to respond.* You're right. It means to do what another person tells us to do. Sometimes when we talk about obeying, we are referring to our parents. How do you obey your parents? *Give the children time to respond.*

Sometimes when we talk about obeying, we think about obeying our teachers. What are some of the rules you must obey in school? *Pause for responses.*

We can also talk about obeying the rules and laws of our community. For example, we have to obey the rules for stop signs and traffic lights. What would happen if we didn't obey the rules for traffic signals? What other rules must we obey for our town or community? *Pause for responses.*

Who's the most important One that we should obey? God! That's right! We need to obey God. There's a story in the Bible about a man who didn't obey God. We'll need some supplies to tell this story in a fun way. *Hand each child a napkin and a resealable bag with crackers.*

Open your Bible to Jonah 1, and show it to the children. In Jonah chapter 1, God wanted Jonah to go to Nineveh to tell the people about him. Jonah didn't want to go, so he disobeyed God. He tried to hide from God and run away from God by getting on a boat that was sailing away. Place your napkin on the floor near you. That will be our water. Get out your square cracker and place it on the napkin. Who can guess what our cracker represents? Right—that's our boat. Now put the bear-shaped crackers on the boat. That's going to be Jonah and the other men on the boat. Put your fish crackers around the boat, on the napkin, as fish in the sea.

Slowly pull your napkin just a little. Jonah and the boat were traveling on the water. Suddenly, a terrible storm came up. Jonah knew he was to blame for the storm because he disobeyed God. He told the men to throw him overboard. When he splashed into the water, a huge fish swallowed him! Why don't you eat one of your bear crackers and we'll pretend that a giant fish gobbled up Jonah! The fish swallowed Jonah whole, but it's not a good idea for us to swallow these crackers whole.

How do you think Jonah felt inside the belly of the fish? What do you think it looked like in there? Do you think it was wet? cold? cramped? *Pause for children's responses.* Rock back and forth and pretend you're the giant fish swimming in the sea. Do you think Jonah got seasick in the fish? *Pause for responses.*

I don't know if Jonah got seasick or not. It probably didn't feel so good being inside the dark, smelly belly of a fish. He probably was thinking, "If I'd just obeyed God and done what he wanted me to do, I wouldn't be in this mess right now!" What else do you think Jonah might have thought while inside the fish? *Pause for children's responses.* When God let Jonah out of the belly of that fish, he obeyed God and went to Nineveh. We need to obey God too.

Thank you for helping me tell the story with your crackers. Please put your crackers back inside your bag. You may snack on them later, to help you remember about today's story. Let's pray.

❤ Dear God, please help me to obey you. Please help me to obey your Word and do what is right. Help me also to obey others—my parents, my teachers, and the laws and rules of my community. Thank you for loving me, just as you loved Jonah. Amen. ❤

Questions Kids Ask About the
New Testament

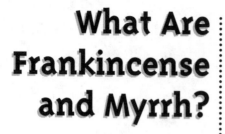

What Are Frankincense and Myrrh?

THEME

We can give gifts to Jesus.

BIBLE REFERENCE
Matthew 2:1-11

SIMPLE SUPPLIES
You'll need a Bible and several aromatic items such as incense, perfume, spices, fruits, or candles.

What's your favorite smell? What are some things that smell bad? *Pass around the items and allow the children time to sniff each item.*

There's a story in the Bible that tells about some smelly gifts! *Open your Bible to Matthew 2, and show it to the children.* In Matthew 2:1-11, we learn about the gifts that Jesus received when he was young. Some wise men presented Jesus with gifts of gold, frankincense, and myrrh.

We all know what gold is. I'd love to be able to give you some real gold, but that would be too expensive. Jesus was also given the gifts of frankincense and myrrh. Both of these gifts had a very strong smell. Frankincense is a type of incense, and when it's burned, it has a nice smell. Myrrh comes from a plant and has a smell like perfume.

The gifts of frankincense and myrrh were gifts with good smells. During this special time of year, Christmastime, we smell lots of wonderful aromas. What are things we often smell at Christmas? *Pause for responses.*

When you get a whiff of a delicious "Christmas-y" smell, remember the wise men's "smelly" gifts. The wise men gave Jesus gifts to honor him. We can give gifts to Jesus too. Our gifts don't always have to be things. Our gifts to Jesus can be kind words said to a friend or family member, or to clean our rooms without grumbling or complaining. Help me think of more gifts we can give to Jesus. *Give the children time to respond.* Let's give these gifts to Jesus this week!

Let's pray. ♥ Dear God, help me remember that I can give gifts to Jesus too. Thank you for the gift of your Son. Amen. ♥

Did Jesus Have to Go to School?

THEME

We need to learn and grow in faith.

BIBLE REFERENCE
Luke 2:41-52

SIMPLE SUPPLIES
You'll need a Bible and a growth chart.

Did you know that Jesus was once a child like you? Jesus grew wiser and older as he was on earth. I need all of you to help with a short game that will help us understand the story about Jesus as a boy. *Ask for one volunteer to leave the immediate area or close his or her eyes. Hide the growth chart somewhere in the room. Tell the remaining children they will state "hot" when the volunteer comes close to finding the chart or "cold" when the volunteer goes farther away from the hiding spot. Invite the volunteer back into the room or area.*

In just a minute we're going to play a little game of lost and found, but first, let's take a peek at a story about Jesus growing up. *Open your Bible to Luke 2:41-52.* What's your favorite holiday? *Allow time for the kids to respond.* Jesus and his family celebrated Jewish holidays or feasts. One of the most important holidays, called Passover, took place in Jerusalem. So, when Jesus was twelve years old, he and his family traveled to Jerusalem and celebrated Passover there. After Passover, on their trip back home, Mary and Joseph realized that Jesus wasn't with them or anyone in the large group they were traveling alongside. You can imagine how upset they were. How many of you have ever been left behind somewhere or lost sometime? *Allow the children to respond.*

Now we want our volunteer to find something lost in this room. We'll give you clues of "hot" when you're near the spot where it's hidden and "cold" when you're farther away from the item. *Have the children give clues as the volunteer looks for the growth chart.* How long did it take you to find the chart? What made it easy or hard to find it? *Allow time for the kids to respond.* It took Jesus' parents *three* days to find him, so you can imagine they were very upset. But, when they did find him, he was sitting with the teachers in the Temple courts, asking them questions. *Read Luke 2:47 aloud.* People were beginning to realize that Jesus was no ordinary boy! The Bible tells us that Jesus went home with his parents and obeyed them. It also says, "Jesus grew in wisdom and stature, and in favor with God and men."

Hold up the growth chart for the children to see. Jesus can relate to you—he had to grow and learn like every kid. What kinds of things do you think Jesus did to grow in his faith? What kinds of things can you do to grow in your faith? *Allow time for the kids to respond.*

Let's pray together. ♥ Dear God, thank you that Jesus can relate to being a kid. Thank you for such an understanding and wise Savior. Amen. ♥

Why Did John the Baptist Eat Such Yucky Food?

THEME

God takes care of those who follow him.

BIBLE REFERENCE

Matthew 3:1-12

SIMPLE SUPPLIES

You'll need a Bible; gummy worms; blindfolds; and three or four lunch bags with various edible treats in them that children will like, such as cereal, chocolate candy bars, or potato chips.

I need some brave volunteers to put on a blindfold, guess the edible contents in one of these bags, and eat it. *Blindfold volunteers, and have them smell, taste, and eat the edible treats. Take off the blindfolds, and ask each one to guess what it was that he or she ate.*

Those were pretty good things to eat, wouldn't you say? What if instead of the chocolate bar, I gave you chocolate covered ants? *Allow time for the kids to respond.* Believe it or not, there are some places where that's considered a treat! How many of you know what escargot is? *Allow kids to respond.* Escargot is snails. How about caviar? Caviar is fish eggs. Snails and fish eggs don't sound too good to some people, but to others they're the finest of foods. Have you ever had a time when you didn't care what your food tasted like? *Let children respond.* You usually don't care about those things when you're focused on something more important.

John the Baptist was a man who didn't worry about what he ate or wore because he had something more important on his mind and in his heart. *Open your Bible and read Matthew 3:1-6.* What seemed to matter the most to John the Baptist? *Allow time for the kids to respond.* John loved God and he loved people. Even Jesus asked to be baptized by John. And John didn't die from eating bugs—God took care of him out there in the desert. God takes care of those who follow him. So the next time you're tempted to worry about what you're going to eat or wear, change your focus to what concerns God, and see how well he takes care of your needs.

Who knows where a fat, roasted tarantula is a treat? (Cambodia) How about where people gather moth caterpillars and roast them around a campfire? (Central Australia) And we like stir-fried meat and vegetables, but did you know that in Indonesia, children catch dragonflies for a tasty stir-fry served on rice? Would you like to eat worms? What about gummy worms?

I'm going to give each of you a gummy worm to remind you that when we follow God, he takes care of us—no matter what kinds of foods we eat! *Pass out gummy worms to each child. You may want to have bug stickers available for any children with dietary restrictions.*

Let's pray together. ♥ Dear God, help us to follow John's example of doing what's really important. Thanks for taking care of our needs when we focus on following you. Amen. ♥

Why Were the Pharisees Always So Mean to Jesus?

THEME

Jesus is God.

BIBLE REFERENCE

Matthew 22:15-22

SIMPLE SUPPLIES

You'll need a Bible, a cooler with ice cubes, paper towels, and pennies.

Has anyone here ever seen ice before? *Allow kids to respond.* That may seem like a silly question to you, but there are people in the world who have never seen an ice cube before. *Hand out ice cubes and paper towels.* Hold the ice for a while. What happens? If you knew someone who had never seen ice, how could you explain what it is? *Allow time for the kids to respond. Collect what's left of the ice.*

For someone who has never seen ice, it would be hard to believe that water can turn into something different. This reminds me of people who could see Jesus, but had a hard time believing that Jesus is God. The Pharisees were a group of leaders who lived during Bible times, and they struggled with believing Jesus. They were mean to Jesus and at times tried to corner him with trick questions. Let's take a look at one of those times.

Open your Bible to Matthew 22:15. Matthew 22:15 says, "Then the Pharisees went out and laid plans to trap him in his words." The Pharisees tried to trap Jesus by asking him a trick question about paying taxes to Caesar. But Jesus beat them at their game by giving them a fantastic answer. *Give pennies to the children.* Whose picture is on the penny? *Allow time for the kids to respond.* Jesus asked them whose picture was on their coins. At that time it wasn't Abraham Lincoln, but Caesar whose picture was on coins. Then Jesus said that they should give to Caesar what is his and give to God what is his. Verse 22 says, "When [the Pharisees] heard this, they were amazed. So they left him and went away." Jesus was not only creative with his answer, he was perfect with it—showing that he was truly God. Instead of seeing the truth about Jesus, though, the Pharisees became more angry.

Why is it important to believe that Jesus is God? What do you think keeps people from believing that Jesus is God even today? How can you help other people learn about Jesus? *Let children respond.* Because Jesus is God, we can trust in his power and know that he will care for us.

Let's pray together. ♥ Dear God, thank you for letting us get to know you in person through Jesus. Thank you that you give us faith to believe that Jesus is God. Amen. ♥

If Jesus Liked Children So Much, Why Didn't He Have Any?

THEME

Jesus had a special purpose on earth.

BIBLE REFERENCE

Mark 10:13-16

SIMPLE SUPPLIES

You'll need a Bible; craft sticks; chenille wires; and a large bag with a hanky, birdseed in a small shakable container, a large book, Frisbee, hat, and a pair of sunglasses inside.

''ve got some ordinary items that have special purposes I'd like for us to look at together. *Open the bag and ask a volunteer to pull out one item. Discuss together the item's special purpose, and then think of other ways the item could be used. For example, the special purpose of the hanky is for blowing noses, but it may also be used as a temporary bandage, to tie back hair, or as a rag.*

You all are very creative thinkers and also did a great job deciding what each thing's special purpose is. Jesus had a special purpose here on earth—to be our Savior. Because of his purpose, his life didn't look like everyone else's. He didn't get married and he didn't have children—but he sure did love kids.

In fact, there was a very busy time in Jesus' ministry when people wanted Jesus to heal them, teach them, help them, and save them. The disciples realized how much was demanded of Jesus and so they became a little protective and selective. When some people came to Jesus and wanted him to hold and bless their children, the disciples shooed them away. But Jesus actually scolded his disciples for keeping the children away, since kids have the kind of believing hearts that can be an example to all people.

Open your Bible to Mark 10:16. Mark 10:16 says, "And he took the children in his arms, put his hands on them and blessed them." I don't know whose hugs you love the most, but think about being hugged by Jesus. In a sense Jesus still hugs you. What are some ways that you feel blessed, loved, or hugged by Jesus? *Allow the kids to respond.* Jesus had a very important purpose here on earth. Jesus' purpose included loving kids so much that he hugged them and he even died on the cross for them.

Pass out two craft sticks and one chenille wire to each child. What's the special purpose of these sticks? *Allow the kids to respond.* We're going to use them to make a cross. The wires are bendable like arms. Let's twist them around the sticks like a huge hug from Jesus and make a cross. Use this as a reminder that Jesus loves you so much that he came for the special purpose of being your Savior.

Let's pray together. ♥ Dear God, thank you for Jesus' special purpose here on earth. Thank you for his love for children then and now. Amen. ♥

Did Jesus Pick Up the Tables After He Knocked Them Over?

THEME

Jesus has God's authority.

BIBLE REFERENCE
John 2:12-25

SIMPLE SUPPLIES
You'll need a Bible, toy sheriff badge, and stars cut from poster board about the size of the sheriff's badge.

Let's play a game of Mother May I? Since I'm the one in charge, let's call it [Your name] May I? and everyone will do what I say. *Line up the children, and let them take turns asking your permission for everyone to take a certain number and type of steps. Give permission as you like. For example, "Pastor Bill, may we take four giant steps toward you?" "No, you all may take one baby step toward me." After a couple of rounds, ask a child to take your place, and continue the game.*

This game actually wasn't about winning or losing. It was about who was in charge. Who *was* in charge? Why did you obey our volunteer when I let this person lead the game? *Allow the children to respond.* Being in charge is called having authority. I gave my authority in this game to someone else. Jesus has God's authority because he is God's Son. Let's see an example of this from the Bible.

Open your Bible to John 2:12-25. There was a time when Jesus went to the Temple in Jerusalem and found people cheating others out of their money. Jesus was angry for their dishonest dealings, but also for the way they were using God's house. In fact, he was so angry that he tipped over the tables and chased those people away. We know that Jesus was perfect so he didn't do it in out-of-control anger. What makes it OK that Jesus did it? *Allow time for the kids to respond.* Jesus has God's authority, and sometimes that means punishment or stopping people who hurt others. We also know that Jesus was considerate, so maybe he picked up the tables sometime later, or maybe he left the tables down so people could think about what they had done as they picked them up. We do know that people needed to be corrected for doing wrong, and Jesus has God's authority to correct them.

Pull out the sheriff badge and put it on. Sometimes a sheriff has deputies. What's the difference between a sheriff and his or her deputies? *Allow the children to respond.* Deputies have the authority that a sheriff gives them. We can be like deputies who carry out God's work—not to tip over tables, but to love and serve. Just as deputies obey the sheriff, we obey Jesus. What are some actions and attitudes that show you're obeying Jesus? *Allow time for the kids to respond. Pass out the star badges to each child.*

Take this badge as a reminder that we're to obey God's authority as a deputy obeys a sheriff. Later you can use a marker or crayon to put your name on it if you want.

Let's pray together. ❤ Dear God, thank you that Jesus has your authority and uses it for the good of all. Help us to respect him and others you've placed in authority. Amen. ❤

Why Did Jesus Tell So Many Stories?

THEME

We can learn how to live from Jesus' stories.

BIBLE REFERENCE
Mark 4:1-20

SIMPLE SUPPLIES
You'll need a Bible, teddy bear, three adhesive bandages, several of your favorite children's books, several bowls of flower seeds, and paper cups partially filled with potting soil.

How many of you like to hear a good story? *Let children respond.* I like stories too! Here are some books that look like they would be interesting. *Pass the books among the children.* Which one of these books looks most interesting to you? Have you read any of these? Do you like them? *Let the children respond.*

One story I like is about a bear who had his *own* way of doing things! He probably looked something like this bear. *Set the teddy bear on your knee.* This bear was named Upstart because he liked to climb up and up. Every time that I say "up," you stretch your arms to the sky. Upstart climbed up *(pause for children to stretch)* hills, trees, and cabins. He climbed up *(pause for children to stretch)* the abandoned wagon that had been left in the woods. Upstart even tried to climb up *(pause for children to stretch)* his daddy's back, but his father wasn't too happy about that.

One day, some men with big boots and equipment on their belts came to the place where Upstart and his family lived. Upstart watched as the men hung thick wires from tree to tree. That night, while eating honey and toast, Upstart told his mother about the men. Upstart's mother knew at once what they had been doing and she warned the children not to climb the trees where the men had hung wire. But Upstart didn't listen to his mother! After all, he did things his *own* way! Upstart could think of nothing else but climbing up *(pause for children to stretch)* one of those trees!

The next day, Upstart sneaked to the place where the men had been. He picked out the tallest tree and looked up *(pause for children to stretch).* Upstart took a deep breath and put one paw, then a second paw, and a third paw on the tree. Upstart stopped. He felt something that hurt! For the first time, he noticed the metal spikes that the men had driven into the tree to use as footholds. That was why the men had worn such big boots! Those spikes weren't meant for tender bear paws, and Upstart fell from the tree.

He hobbled home, crying all the way. Upstart's mother put bandages on his three hurt paws. *Let children help you put adhesive bandages on three of the teddy bear's paws.* What could Upstart have done differently? *Allow children to respond.* If Upstart had obeyed, he might not have hurt himself. Did you learn anything from listening to the story about Upstart? *Allow children to respond.* It's not cool to disobey, is it? Stories are a good way to learn things.

Open your Bible to Mark 4:1-20. The Bible says in Mark 4:2, "[Jesus] taught them many things by parables." A parable is a story. Jesus told stories so that the people could learn from them. In Mark 4:1-20, Jesus told a story about a man who planted seeds in bad soil. Some of the seeds didn't even get to grow into plants because birds ate them. Then there were the poor little plants that tried to grow but became weak and withered. The man also planted seeds where there were weeds. What do you suppose happened to the baby plants that tried to grow among the weeds? *Allow children to respond.* That's right, the weeds took all the sunshine and water from the baby plants there. Then the man planted seeds in good soil. Those plants had plenty of rich nutrients from the soil, water, and sunshine. They grew to be healthy and strong. Jesus used this story to teach that it's important for seeds to have the things they need to grow—and it's important for God's children to have what we need to grow spiritually. *Distribute the paper cups with soil, and place the seeds where kids can reach them.* What can we do to grow in the Lord? *Allow children to answer.* We need to read the Bible, don't we? Plant one seed in your cup for Bible study. *Guide children in placing one seed slightly below the soil's surface.* Singing songs of praise helps us grow close to the Lord. Let's plant a second seed for worshipping through music. *Allow children to plant the second seed.* And we can tell others about Jesus. Let's plant a seed for that. *Children should plant the third seed.* Jesus used the story about the seeds to teach us how to grow spiritually. And Jesus' stories teach many other lessons as well. We can learn how to live from Jesus' stories.

💜 Dear Jesus, thank you for all the wonderful stories that you told. We can learn so much from them. Thank you for the Bible where we can find your stories. Amen. 💜

Take home your cup, and set it in a sunny place. You can water the seeds a little every day. As you watch your plants grow, thank Jesus for stories that teach us how to live.

What Makes Jesus Laugh?

THEME

Jesus understands what life is like for us.

BIBLE REFERENCE

John 1:1-14

SIMPLE SUPPLIES

You'll need a Bible and a stopwatch.

How many of you like to exercise? *Allow children to respond.* I brought my stopwatch. Let's run in place for twenty seconds. Ready? Go! *Run in place with children for twenty seconds.* Stop! That was great! My head's clear! My heart's pounding! How do you feel? *Allow children to answer.*

Let's try that again for forty-five seconds. Go! *Run in place with children for forty-five seconds.* Stop! I'm breathing hard this time. Are you? Anybody tired? Anyone sweating? *Let the children offer their comments as they are seated.*

Some of you are tired. Some of you aren't. Some of you are sweating. Some of you aren't. We're all different, but in some things, we're alike. What are a few ways you're different from those around you? What are a few ways we're like each other? *Allow children to answer.*

Open your Bible to John 1:1-14. The Bible tells us that Jesus was God's Son but that he also was human. Listen to verses 1 and 14 from the first chapter of John. *Read these verses aloud.* In this passage, the Word is Jesus. Jesus was with God in the beginning, Jesus is God, and Jesus lived on earth with us. Since Jesus lived on earth as a man, he got hungry. He got tired. He laughed. He probably even got sweaty.

It's important to know that Jesus is God and was also a man. We can be sure that whatever we face, Jesus faced it too. What are things that tempt you that might have tempted Jesus when he was a boy? What are things you feel that Jesus might have felt? *Let children respond.* Jesus felt pain like we do. When do we feel pain? When have you been hurt and felt pain? *Let children respond.* When Jesus was nailed to the cross, the pain was terrible!

Jesus understands our temptations and our hurts. He also understands what makes us happy. What might have made Jesus laugh? *Allow children to respond.* Who can show me something that makes *you* happy? *Explain that you'd like the volunteer to act out that thing. Allow several volunteers to pantomime things that make them happy.*

Jesus lived on earth as a man. He was hungry. He felt pain. He cried. He even laughed. Jesus understands how life is for us because he was a man. When we have questions about life, we can talk to Jesus by praying. Let's talk to him now.

♥ Dear Jesus, we're so thankful for your love. Even though you are the Son of God, you chose to be a man, too. It's wonderful to know that you understand what life is like. We can talk to you about anything. Amen. ♥

Did Jesus Just Pretend to Be Asleep Before He Calmed the Storm?

THEME

We can trust Jesus.

BIBLE REFERENCE

Matthew 8:23-27

SIMPLE SUPPLIES

You'll need a Bible, a picture of a starry night, a picture of a sunshiny day, clothespins, green construction paper leaves in a grocery bag, a black marker, and a branch that's been stuck securely in a pot of soil.

like to think of myself as a really good helper. Are you good helpers? What kinds of things can you do to help? *Let kids respond.* You are good helpers.

Let's look at this picture of a starry night. *Show the picture.* Do you think Jesus needs our help to place all the stars in the sky? *Let the children offer responses.* Well, what about the sun? *Show a picture of a sunshiny day.* Does Jesus need our help holding up the sun? *Allow the children to respond.* You're right. Jesus doesn't need our help with either of those things. Jesus has these things under control.

I wonder if Jesus could use our help to grow things. I have a branch here that I thought I'd use to grow a tree. *Point to the branch in the pot.* I also brought some leaves that I made. They're in this grocery bag. *Open the bag.* Can you help me put these leaves on my tree? *Pass out the clothespins, and guide the children in pinning the paper leaves on the tree.*

That looks like a great tree. Do you think it will grow bigger? Why not? *Let children comment.* I suppose you're right. I can't make things grow. But I don't need to! Jesus has that under control. Jesus has everything under his control. Let me show you what I mean.

Open your Bible to Matthew 8:23-27, and read it aloud.

Jesus wasn't worried about a storm. He was so at ease that he was taking a nap! Why do you suppose Jesus knew everything would be OK? *Allow children to respond.* Jesus wasn't worried because he knew it was all under control. While Jesus lived on earth, he healed the sick and raised the dead. Jesus knew he could handle a storm. The wind and waves were nothing to him.

The disciples didn't need to be afraid. They had watched him perform all sorts of miracles. They should have trusted Jesus to take care of the storm. Instead, they were frightened. Maybe the disciples should have remembered who makes starry skies and sunlit days. And maybe they should have thought about who makes things grow. The disciples should have remembered who had things under control. They wouldn't have been afraid if they had trusted Jesus.

There may be things in *our* lives that are bigger than we can control. But we don't have to be afraid—no matter how big or scary some things may seem. God can take care of us. Sometimes God uses our parents to help us, and sometimes he uses friends or other people who guide us. Jesus will take control. And *nothing* is too big for Jesus.

Use a marker to write "JESUS" across the front of the grocery bag, and then remove one construction paper leaf from the tree in the pot. What is something that's too big to control without Jesus? *Allow a child to offer a response. Use the marker to write the response on the leaf. Then hand the leaf to the child who volunteered the response.* Why don't you give this to Jesus? Drop it in the bag. It's in Jesus' bag now. It's his to control. You can count on Jesus to take care of this. *Take another leaf from the tree and repeat the activity, continuing as long as children offer responses.*

Let's pray. ❤ Dear Jesus, we know you can calm the sea, heal the sick, and make things grow. You're in control of the universe, even placing the stars and the sun in the sky. When we feel afraid, we know that we can turn to you and to the people you put in our lives to take care of us. We can trust you to always have everything under control. Amen. ❤

What Did Jesus Do With All the Leftover Food After He Fed Five Thousand People?

THEME

Jesus is glad when we share with others.

BIBLE REFERENCE
John 6:1-14

SIMPLE SUPPLIES
You'll need a Bible and a loaf of uncut bread.

Isn't it nice when someone has something really good and decides to share? I have something that I want to share with you—a loaf of delicious bread. There's only one piece, but it's a really big piece so we can all tear off bite-sized pieces. *Allow children to pinch off pieces of bread.* What do you think about this bread? Does it taste good? Was it fun to share the bread? *Let the children offer comments.*

Jesus believed in sharing. *Open your Bible to John 6:1-14, and read this aloud.*

The little boy shared something good—he shared his lunch. And when Jesus prayed over the food, one little boy's lunch became a miracle. We might wonder what Jesus and the disciples did with the food that was left over. The Bible doesn't say. Perhaps Jesus had the disciples take the baskets of leftovers to the poor. Maybe the food was sent to the homeless people who sat outside the city gates. We don't know for sure. But we do know that Jesus believed in sharing.

Jesus is glad when we share with others because good things happen when people share. What are things we can share in our homes? What are things we can share with others at school? at church? How do you plan on sharing today? *Let children respond to each question.*

We can share things we have, we can share love, and we can share through our attitudes. Jesus and this boy in the Bible are great examples for us to follow!

Let's pray. ❤ Dear Jesus, thank you for teaching us about sharing. We want to share because we know it makes you glad. Good things happen when people share. Amen. ❤

Did Jesus Walk on the Moon?

THEME

Jesus can do anything.

BIBLE REFERENCE

Matthew 14:22-33

SIMPLE SUPPLIES

You'll need a Bible, flip-flops, sandals, tennis shoes, and hiking boots.

I believe in having the right equipment for whatever I plan to do! That goes for walking, too. What would these shoes be the right equipment for? *Hold flip-flops while kids respond.* Flip-flops are just the thing for walking to the pool! *Hold up the sandals.* What about these? What are these for? I wear sandals for walks on the beach because I like to feel the sand squishing between my toes. *Hold the tennis shoes.* What about these shoes? What are they good for? *Hold up the boots.* And these shoes? What are they for? Hiking is the ultimate form of walking! These boots make you feel that your feet are really protected, don't they? What other kinds of shoes might be good equipment for me to add to my collection? How will they help me? What kind of shoes would I need to walk on water? *Let kids respond.*

You're right in thinking that I can't walk on water—no matter what kind of shoes I have. But Jesus can do anything, and Jesus did walk on water! Jesus had been doing a lot of preaching and he wanted to rest. So he sent the disciples to get a boat while he told the people goodbye. Let's see what happened. *Read Matthew 14:22-33 aloud.* What do you think the disciples thought when they saw someone walking on the water? What would you think if you saw someone walking on water? *Allow children to respond.*

What do you suppose the disciples learned about Jesus that day? *Allow children to answer.* They learned that Jesus was powerful. A lake full of water didn't stop Jesus. What do you think could stop Jesus? *Allow children to respond.* Nothing can stop Jesus. I am sure that if he wanted to, Jesus could even walk on the moon. And he wouldn't need special shoes!

The disciples learned that Jesus could do *anything*. What about today? Do you think Jesus can *still* do anything? *Allow children time to respond.*

❤ Dear Jesus, how powerful and mighty you are! You can do anything. Thank you that you love us. We are thrilled to know that the one who walks on water cares for us. We worship you. Amen. ❤

Did Everyone Like Zacchaeus After He Met Jesus?

THEME

God likes us.

BIBLE REFERENCE

Luke 19:1-9

SIMPLE SUPPLIES

You'll need a large bowl, a mixing spoon, plastic spoons, napkins, unsweetened chocolate (one ounce per six children, melted in the bowl just prior to the lesson), and a bag of sugar.

How many of you like chocolate? *Allow time for responses.* Earlier today I melted some chocolate in this bowl. *Show the bowl of melted chocolate, and let children smell it.* Doesn't this look delicious? I'd like to share it with all of you. *Make sure the chocolate isn't too hot. Pass out spoons and napkins, and allow children to take a spoonful of chocolate from the bowl to eat. Upon tasting, they will probably respond with disgust.*

Do you like the chocolate? Why or why not? What's wrong with it? *Allow time for responses.* The chocolate I gave you is unsweetened. It doesn't have any sugar in it. I'm going to give each of you a new spoon. *Collect the dirty spoons, pass out clean spoons, and set out a bag of sugar.* Take a spoonful of sugar, and put it into the bowl of chocolate. *Have children each add a spoonful of sugar. When they're done, stir the sugar into the chocolate.*

How do you think this mixture will taste? Who wants to try it? *Allow willing children to taste the new mixture.* How does it taste? Why did you want to taste it? Why didn't you want to taste it?

Open your Bible to Luke 19:1-9. This chocolate reminds me of a man from the Bible named Zacchaeus who stole money from people. The townspeople didn't like him at all, just as we didn't like the bitter chocolate. But Jesus liked him and even went to Zacchaeus' house. Because of Jesus' love and kindness, Zacchaeus followed Jesus, stopped stealing, and even paid back the money he'd stolen.

Do you think all the people liked Zacchaeus after he met Jesus? Why or why not? *Allow time for responses.* Just like some of us might not want to taste the chocolate after having the bitter taste in our mouths, some people were probably afraid of trusting Zacchaeus because of all the bad things he'd done before. Even though Zacchaeus did wrong things, God liked him!

All of us have done things that are wrong. But once we ask God to help us with these things, he'll begin to change our lives! People around you may not trust you right away, but God does. Turn to someone next to you and say, "God likes you!"

♥ Dear God, please help each child here understand how much you like him or her. Please let each one feel how special he or she always is to you. In Jesus' name, amen. ♥

Was Jesus More Popular Than My Favorite Music Group?

THEME

Good friends bring their friends to Jesus.

BIBLE REFERENCE
Mark 2:1-12

SIMPLE SUPPLIES
You'll need a Bible.

Let's do the Bunny Hop! *Pick two child volunteers and teach them how to do the Bunny Hop. Children won't mind if you don't know exactly how to do the Bunny Hop. Just have the two volunteers line up behind you and follow along as you kick out your legs and hop. Encourage the others to hum along as you hop. Then have the two volunteers each pick someone else to join them, and hum and hop again. Continue until all children are hopping.*

What did you like about the Bunny Hop? What did you like about bringing a friend along to hop with you? Have you ever brought your friends along to do something else fun that you were doing? If so, what happened? *Allow time for responses.*

A story from the book of Mark in the Bible tells us of some friends who brought their paralyzed friend along with them. Being paralyzed means that you cannot move your own body. *Read Mark 2:1-5 aloud.* Why did the friends have to lower the paralyzed man through the roof? Why do you think so many people wanted to be around Jesus? How did Jesus get to be so popular? Do you think Jesus was more popular than your favorite music group? *Allow time for responses to each question.*

Many people wanted to be near Jesus, and many friends took their friends to see Jesus. Have you ever brought a friend to church with you or talked with him or her about God's love? When? How did your friend respond? *Allow time for responses to each question.* Are there times you didn't share God with others when you could have? What happened? Why did you choose not to share about God's love? What are some ways you could bring your friends to Jesus? *Allow time for responses to each question.*

We can pray with our friends, we can show them God's love by the way we love and accept others, we can share how much we love Jesus and how much he helps us. There are many ways we can share Jesus.

When we did the Bunny Hop, we brought our friends along to join us. Good friends bring their friends along to do fun things. Good friends also bring their friends to Jesus.

♥ Dear Jesus, please help each of us think of one way we can bring our friends to you. Please give us the courage and excitement to share you with others this week. In Jesus' name, amen. ❤

Note: If you're unfamiliar with the Bunny Hop song actions, you may do the motions to another familiar song. The Bunny Hop moves are as follows: right leg out twice, left leg out twice, hop forward once, hop backward once, hop forward three times. Participants stand in a line with their hands on the waist of the person in front of them.

Why Did Peter Get Into So Much Trouble?

THEME

God loves us even when we make mistakes.

BIBLE REFERENCE

Matthew 26:69-75

SIMPLE SUPPLIES

You'll need a Bible and one or more paddle-ball toys.

H*old up a paddle-ball toy.* How many of you have played with one of these before? What does the elastic string do when you hit the ball? Let's test it. *Invite one or more children to test the paddle balls. Let children take turns with the toys, then collect the paddle balls.* What happened to the ball each time you hit it? Did the ball ever keep going and not come back toward you? *Let children respond.*

Demonstrate with the paddle ball as you speak. Each time I hit the ball away from me, it comes back. The elastic string always returns the ball. It doesn't necessarily always hit the paddle again, but it does come back toward me. This reminds me of Christ's love for us. No matter where we go or what we do, Jesus always loves us.

The Bible tells us about a man named Peter who loved Jesus very much. He made a promise that he would never turn his back on Jesus. Jesus knew Peter was full of good ideas, but he also knew Peter made mistakes. Jesus told Peter, "This very night, before the rooster crows, you will disown me three times" (Matthew 26:34). Peter didn't believe Jesus.

A short while later, Jesus was arrested. Let's read what happened. *Read Matthew 26:69-75 aloud.* What Jesus had said came true! Peter felt bad about his actions, but the story doesn't end here. Later in the Bible, we learn about Peter telling many people about Jesus. He wasn't afraid to tell others about Jesus, and he was even sent to jail because of his love for Jesus. And God used Peter to begin the first churches.

How do you think Jesus felt about Peter after the rooster crowed? How do you think Peter felt after the rooster crowed? How do you think Jesus feels about you when you make mistakes? *Let children respond to each question.*

Even though Peter made a big mistake in saying that he didn't know Jesus, Jesus still loved Peter. No matter how bad we mess up or how far from God we may get, God always loves us and wants us back—just like the ball on the elastic string. No matter how hard we may hit it away from the paddle, the elastic string always brings it back. God does that with us. No matter how much we may mess up, God always loves us and wants us back.

♥ Dear Jesus, thank you that you love us even when we make mistakes. Please help us understand that nothing we could ever do could make you stop loving us. In Jesus' name, amen. ♥

If time permits, give the children opportunities to play with the paddle balls again to reinforce today's teaching. Talk with the children as they play, and relate their play to today's lesson.

Did God Forget About Jesus When He Was on the Cross?

THEME
God hears us when we cry.

BIBLE REFERENCE
Mark 15:33-41

SIMPLE SUPPLIES
You'll need a Bible, two disposable cups, string, scissors, and beads or washers. Before the lesson make a "telephone" by poking a small hole in
the bottom of each of the cups. Cut one ten-foot length of string, and thread it through the hole in the bottom of one cup. Tie a washer or bead to the end of the string inside the cup. Repeat this process with the other end of the string and the other cup.

Can you guess what these cups and string are for? *Give time for responses.* I've made something like a telephone with them. Let's see how it works. *Choose two volunteers. Have each child hold a cup and carefully walk away from each other until the string is taught. Then as one child speaks into one cup, the other holds the cup to listen through it. Have volunteers take turns talking and listening.*

Did my telephone always work? Could you always hear your partner? What made it easier or harder to hear the other person? *Let children respond.* This phone may not have worked perfectly but there is one type of communication that always works! There is one special "call" we can make that will always be heard—our prayers.

Open your Bible to Mark 15. The Bible tells us that many of the leaders during Jesus' time didn't like the things Jesus was saying and doing. They wanted to make him stop saying he was God. But Jesus just kept right on teaching, blessing, and healing the people. Finally the leaders decided to kill Jesus by nailing him to a cross. God knew that Jesus would die this way, but God also knew that Jesus would rise from the dead and live in heaven forever! While Jesus was on the cross, he cried out to God. *Read Mark 15:34 aloud.* God heard Jesus' prayer, but didn't take Jesus down from the cross and save him from death. Instead, he gave Jesus the strength to finish his task.

Have you ever cried out to God? Why? Did you hear or see God's answer? *Allow time for responses.* Sometimes God changes our problems so they're not problems anymore, and sometimes he gives us the strength to make it through the problem. We can never be sure how God will answer our prayers. But one thing is for certain, God always hears us when we cry out to him! God heard Jesus and he hears us, too.

♥ Dear God, thank you for always listening to our prayers. Please help us remember to cry out to you when things are good and when things are bad. Thank you for always being there for us. We love you. Amen. ♥

If time permits, let children experiment more with the "telephone."

Why Didn't Jesus Just Use His Power to Get Down From the Cross?

THEME

Jesus gave himself for us.

BIBLE REFERENCE
Luke 23:33-43

SIMPLE SUPPLIES
You'll need a Bible, an adult helper, masking tape, and a superhero costume (or sweatpants and shirt that can be stuffed with towels or newspaper to look like muscles).

*P*rior to the lesson, have your helper dress up as a muscle-bound superhero, then have this person stay out of sight. Using masking tape on the ground, mark off an area where you can play a game of tag. Also, mark a 5x5-foot square that will serve as "jail."

Today we're going to play Hobble Tag. Stand up and put your knees together. Now try to walk. This is how you'll be allowed to move around during the game. As you can see, there are masking tape boundaries drawn on the floor. During our game of Tag, you may not go outside these lines. If you go outside the boundaries or get tagged, you must go to the jail box. *Point out the jail box.* I will be "It," and I can walk or run normally. Let's play!

Play Tag until all the children are in jail. Then have your volunteer suddenly burst out from the hiding place. You may try to capture the superhero but this person is impervious to your assaults. Have the superhero walk into the jail and set all the captives free, saying, "I will take your place, you may go free!" The game is now over. While your superhero sits in jail, seat the children for discussion time.

What was different or unusual about this game of Tag? What was the superhero all about? Can you think of anyone else who's like our superhero? *Let children answer.* This superhero reminds me of Jesus.

The Bible tells us that after Jesus had been teaching the people for about three years, some religious leaders decided that they were going to kill Jesus. They had Jesus arrested, and soldiers took him away. Jesus was nailed on a cross and left to die. Jesus did this as a way of taking our punishment on himself, just like the superhero went to jail for you in our game. While he was on the cross, Jesus cried out to God. Some soldiers watching this made fun of Jesus and teased that if he was really God's Son he should just use his power to get down from the cross. Listen to what they said. *Read Luke 23:35-39 aloud.* But that wasn't God's plan.

Jesus had all the power in the world yet he died on the cross. Do you think he could have gotten himself down? Why or why not? Why do you think Jesus didn't take himself down from the cross? *Allow time for responses.* When we sin we must be punished. That punishment is death. Jesus had never done anything wrong and didn't need to be punished. When Jesus died, he took the punishment for all *our* sins. He died so that we could have forgiveness for our sins and so that we could be close to God. Jesus gave himself for us.

Our superhero has stayed in jail ever since you were set free. Did Jesus stay dead? *Allow time for responses.* Jesus rose to life again and lives in heaven forever. Take a minute to think of a sin in your life that you need God's forgiveness for. Pretend to put that sin in your fist. *Have the superhero go through the group pretending to take the sins from the children's hands.* Jesus is the real superhero who takes away our sin and lets us be close to God.

❤ Dear God, thank you for sending Jesus to die so that we could be close to you and be forgiven of our sins. We love Jesus and we love you! Amen. ❤

Does Jesus Still Have Holes in His Hands?

THEME

When we believe that Jesus is the Son of God, we can have eternal life.

BIBLE REFERENCE
John 20:24-31

SIMPLE SUPPLIES
You'll need a Bible and a box of facial tissues. It would also be helpful to have one or two teenage or adult helpers.

L et's play a quick game. Find three or four friends, and sit in a circle with them. *Pause for children to get into groups, and have one adult or teenager stand nearby.* The object of this game is for each group to keep the tissue from touching the ground, but you can't touch it with any part of your body. *Give each volunteer a tissue to hold above the middle of each circle of children. Then on your command, have the volunteers drop the tissues. The children should blow the tissue around. Play several times.*

That was amazing. I didn't see anything and yet those tissues moved all over. How did that happen? You blew air to move it? But I didn't see the air. How can I know it's really there? What are other things you can't see but know are real? *Let children respond.*

The Bible tells us about one of Jesus' disciples who had trouble believing in things he couldn't see. *Open your Bible to John 20.* Thomas had heard that Jesus was alive again because the other disciples said they had seen Jesus, but Thomas just couldn't believe it. He hadn't seen Jesus, and it just seemed unbelievable.

Then next time Thomas was with all the other disciples, Jesus suddenly appeared—even though the doors were locked! And Jesus still had the marks from the nails and the hole in his side from where the soldiers pierced him with a sword. When Thomas saw Jesus and the marks on his body, he knew it was Jesus, and he called Jesus his Lord and his God. What emotions do you think Thomas felt when he saw Jesus? *Allow children to respond.*

That was wonderful that Thomas was able to finally believe that Jesus was alive again. But Jesus knew that you and I and everyone who has lived since Jesus went back to heaven wouldn't have the chance to see Jesus with our eyes or see the places where he was wounded. Jesus talked about us. He told Thomas that people who have not seen him and yet still believe in him will be blessed. That's you and me!

And God even says why this and other events are recorded in the Bible. He says that they are written so that we will believe that Jesus is the Son of God, and that by believing, we can have eternal life. When we believe that Jesus is the Son of God and that he died to pay for our sins, we will live with God forever in heaven. That is good news. Let's celebrate that good news!

Here's a tissue for each of you. *Have your volunteers hand each child a tissue.* When I say "go," let's all blow our tissues up in the air. *Say "go" and have the children blow their tissues in the air briefly, then have them fold their tissues.*

We can't see air, but we know it's real. We can't see Jesus either, but we know that he is real too.

❤ Dear God, thank you for Jesus. Thank you for telling us all about him so that we can believe in Jesus and live with you forever. In Jesus' name, amen. ❤

Where Is Jesus Now?

THEME

When Jesus went to heaven, he sent the Holy Spirit to be with us.

BIBLE REFERENCE
Acts 1:1-11

SIMPLE SUPPLIES

You'll need a Bible; colorful, interesting picture postcards of vacation places; pieces of heavy paper cut to the size of postcards; and pencils.

When was the last time you went on a vacation? Where did you go? Have you ever sent a postcard to someone while you were on vacation or gotten a postcard from someone who was on a vacation? *Allow children to respond.* People send postcards because they want the people they love to know what it's like where they are and to let their friends know they're thinking of them.

I brought some postcards with me today. *Have the children hand around the postcards.* Aren't the places on the cards beautiful? I know of someplace even more beautiful. It has streets of gold, wonderful trees with delicious fruit on them all year, and no night. Do you know the place I'm talking about? *Allow children to respond.* That's right—heaven. Have you ever gotten a postcard from heaven? *Allow children to respond.* No, I haven't either. But we all have gotten something wonderful from someone who went to heaven.

In the Bible it tells about when Jesus went back to heaven. Jesus had risen from the dead and spent forty days meeting with people and doing wonderful things. But then it was time for him to go to heaven. Acts 1:8-11 tells us what happened next. *Read this passage aloud.*

Jesus went back to heaven. Although Jesus didn't send a postcard of heaven to the people then or to us now, he did send the Holy Spirit. The Holy Spirit does many wonderful things for us. Even though we can't know exactly what it's like in heaven where Jesus is, we can have the Holy Spirit to give us power and comfort.

I have some blank postcards here for you. *Hand out paper and pencils.* On one side of the card, write a prayer of thanks to Jesus for sending the Holy Spirit to us, and later you can draw a picture on the other side of what you think heaven might be like. *Give children time to write their prayers, then pray together.*

❤ Dear Jesus, thank you that you sent the Holy Spirit to us when you went to heaven. Even though we don't have a picture of where you are now, I'm excited to be there with you someday! In your name, amen. ❤

Is the Holy Spirit Inside of Me?

THEME

The Holy Spirit gives us power to tell others about Jesus.

BIBLE REFERENCE

Acts 1:8, 2:1-13; 1 Corinthians 3:16

SIMPLE SUPPLIES

You'll need a Bible, copies of the "Love in Any Language" handout (p. 102), a CD or tape player, CD or tape of speech or songs in a foreign language (look for these at your local library). Or ask someone who's fluent in another language to speak to the children.

What language do you speak? Does anyone here speak a different language? *Allow children to respond.* There are many, many different languages. Let's listen to what a different language sounds like. *Play the CD or tape or have your volunteer speak to the children.* Were you able to understand what was said? Unless you know the language, you can't understand what people are saying when they talk.

The Bible, in the book of Acts, tells about a time when there were many people visiting Jerusalem who had come from all over and spoke many different languages. During this time, a group of Jesus' disciples were together in a room praying. Jesus had gone back to heaven, but before he left he promised to send the Holy Spirit to his disciples. Let's read from Acts 2:1-4 and see what happened. *Read these verses aloud.*

So the disciples were in the room when they heard a sound like a strong wind inside the room. Can you make a sound like a strong wind? *Allow children to make a wind sound.* Then they saw what looked like tiny flames of fire stopping on top of each man's head. Put your hands together, and then hold them on top of your head. That was already pretty amazing, but then something even more amazing happened. The men began to speak in languages other than their own. They were able to talk to all the different people in the town in their own languages and tell them how much Jesus loved them, and how he died and rose again. The disciples knew that the power to do this had come from the Holy Spirit.

Did you know that the Holy Spirit lives inside everyone that believes in Jesus? In 1 Corinthians 3:16 it says, "Don't you know that you yourselves are God's temple, and that God's Spirit lives in you?" That's wonderful news. The powerful Holy Spirit lives inside us, and he wants us to have power too. But this power is for a special purpose. *Read Acts 1:8.* How are we supposed to use this power? *Let children respond.*

How many of you have friends who need to know about Jesus? Do any of your friends speak a different language from you? *Allow children to respond.* Most of your friends speak the same language you do, so the Holy Spirit doesn't need you to speak a different language to tell them about Jesus. But the Holy Spirit will help you know the words to say to your friends as you tell them about Jesus.

I have a handout here with John 3:16 on it in different languages. These may be hard for you to read or understand, but someone from one of these countries could read this and understand what it says about Jesus. Keep these verses to remind you that the Holy Spirit gives us power to tell others about Jesus. *Give each child a "Love in Any Language" handout.*

❤ Dear God, thank you for the Holy Spirit that you send to live in us. Help us to use the power of the Holy Spirit to tell others about Jesus. In Jesus' name, amen. ❤

John 3:16

Love in Any Language

SPANISH:

Porque tanto amó Dios al mundo, que dio a su Hijo unigénito, para que todo el que cree en él no se pierda, sino que tenga vida eterna.

FRENCH:

Car Dieu a tant aimé le monde qu'il a donné son Fils unique, afin que quiconque croit en lui ne périsse point, mais qu'il ait la vie éternelle.

ITALIAN:

Dio infatti ha tanto amato il mondo da dare il suo Figlio unigenito, perché chiunque crede in lui non muoia, ma abbia la vita eterna.

TAGALOG:

Ito ay sapagkat sa ganitong paraan inibig ng Diyos ang sanlibutan kaya ipinagkaloob niya ang kaniyang bugtong na Anak upang ang sinumang sumampalataya sa kaniya ay hindi mapahamak kundi magkaroon ng buhay na walang hanggan.

Did Saul's Horses Go Blind Too?

THEME

When we meet Jesus, our lives are changed.

BIBLE REFERENCE
Acts 9:1-20

SIMPLE SUPPLIES
You'll need a Bible, small pieces of paper, cotton swabs, a small cup of lemon juice, and a lamp with an exposed bulb. If you have more than ten children, you may want to have extra cups of juice and an extra lamp.

Let's talk about how things change. Leaves change in the autumn. Colors change when you mix them. What other things change? *Allow children to respond.* There are lots of things that change. And do you know that people can change too?

The Bible tells us about one man who really changed. He was Saul, and he wasn't a nice man. He hated everyone who believed in Jesus. He hunted for them, and whenever he found Christians, he arrested them and had them thrown in jail. But God had a bigger plan for Saul. He wanted Saul to be a missionary and to go all over the world telling other people that Jesus is God's Son.

Open your Bible to Acts 9. Jesus appeared to Saul while he was on his way to a city called Damascus. A great light from heaven flashed around and Jesus spoke to Saul. Listen to what happened. *Read Acts 9:3-9 aloud.* How would you feel if this happened to you? How do you think Saul felt? How do you think Saul felt when he heard Jesus speak to him after he had been so mean to people who followed Jesus? *Allow children to respond.* The light blinded Saul, but not any of the men with him. Since only Saul was blinded, we can guess that none of the animals, even the horses, were blinded either. God blinded only Saul, because it was Saul he wanted to change. What do you think it's like to be blind? *Allow children to respond.*

Saul did change. He learned that Jesus is God's Son, sent to save everyone from their sins. And the Bible tells us in Acts 9:20, that soon after Saul was healed of his blindness, he started preaching that Jesus is the Son of God. We know him as Paul. And Paul did become a great missionary, and God even used him to write many books in the New Testament.

I want to show you how a light can make things change, just as God made a change in Saul. *Dip a cotton swab in the lemon juice and draw a heart on the paper. Show the paper to the children.* You can't see much of anything on this paper, can you? That was just like Saul's life before he met Jesus. You just couldn't see much good in his life. But God knew Saul would be able to do great things for him. God used light when he talked to Saul. Let's see what a bright light will do to this paper. *Hold the paper near the light bulb. As the paper heats, the lemon juice will darken until you will be able to see the heart shape. Show this to the children, and let each one draw a heart on paper with lemon juice.*

When you get home, your parents can help you hold the paper near a light and watch it change. Keep the changed paper as a reminder that when we meet Jesus, he can change our lives. Jesus can change our hearts so we're more kind to our family members. He can change our hearts to help us show love to people we don't like very much.

♥ Dear God, thank you for sending Jesus. Please let Jesus change my life so I can do the things you want me to do. In Jesus' name, amen. ♥

Why Is the Book of Revelation So Confusing?

THEME

Heaven will be a wonderful place for us.

BIBLE REFERENCE
Revelation 21:1-7, 16-26; 22:1-3

SIMPLE SUPPLIES
You'll need a Bible; paper; yellow or orange markers; and easily recognized symbols such as a stop sign, a Nike swoosh, the golden arches of McDonald's, or perhaps your own church's logo. If you have the resources, it would be fun to provide gold gel pens or gold glitter pens for the children.

I've brought some symbols for us to look at. Symbols represent things or remind us of something. Let's see which of these you recognize. *Hold up one of the symbols.* Does anyone know what this means? *Allow children to respond as you show all your symbols. Explain symbols they don't recognize.* When we know what a symbol represents, it's easy for us to understand. But when we're not sure what it means, it can be confusing. Sometimes the Bible can seem confusing—especially the book of Revelation. Part of the reason this book can seem confusing is because God used symbols in it that we don't clearly understand.

God explained to us some of the symbols used in the book of Revelation. But not everyone agrees on what God meant other symbols to represent. Fortunately, many parts of Revelation are pretty easy to understand. One part of the book tells us about heaven. Who here knows some of what heaven will be like? *Allow the children to respond.* Let me read what Revelation says about heaven. *Read Revelation 21:4, 16-19a, 21-26; 22:1-2.*

What part of heaven do you think you will like best? *Allow children to respond.* Heaven is a special place that God designed for us. The Bible says that only those whose names are written in the Lamb's book of life will be allowed in heaven. Who is the Lamb? *Allow children to respond.* Jesus is the Lamb. That's one of the symbols in the book that we can easily understand. What is the book of life? *Allow children to respond.* That is where Jesus writes our names when we become followers of Jesus. Each one of you can get your name in that special book. When you believe that Jesus is the Son of God, and ask him to forgive you for all the wrong things you've done, he'll forgive you and write your name in his book.

Let's thank God that he has made such a wonderful place for us. ♥ Dear God, we are so excited to think about heaven. Thank you for making such a wonderful place for us, and for sending Jesus so we can go to heaven. In Jesus' name, amen. ❤

I have paper and pens for you to make your own symbol of heaven. Remember that a symbol is not a complete picture of something, but just a simple representation. *Allow the children a few minutes to draw a simple symbol for heaven. Allow a few children to share what they drew with the rest of the group.* Take home these simple symbols of heaven as a reminder that God has a wonderful place waiting for everyone whose name is in the Lamb's book of life.

Scripture Index

OLD TESTAMENT REFERENCES

Genesis 1:1-2 8
Genesis 1:24-28 10
Genesis 2:2-3 12
Genesis 2:19-24 14
Genesis 4:1-8 16
Genesis 6:11–7:5. 18
Genesis 9:8-17 20
Genesis 11:1-9 22
Genesis 15:1-6; 22:17a 24
Genesis 21:1-7 26
Genesis 27:1-40 28
Genesis 37:1-4 30
Genesis 37:5-10; 41:25-32 32
Exodus 5–12 . . . . 34, 36
Exodus 16:1-31. 38
Exodus 32:1-20; 34:1-10. 40
Joshua 6:1-20 42
Judges 16 44
1 Samuel 3:1-11 46
1 Samuel 16:7. . . . . 10, 58
1 Samuel 17 48
1 Samuel 20 50
1 Samuel 24 52
1 Kings 3:1-15. 54
1 Kings 17:1-6. 56
Esther 2. 58
Psalm 121:3b-4. 12
Proverbs 27:19 10
Isaiah 43:10b 8
Jeremiah 32:17 26
Ezekiel 36:26. 10
Daniel 3 60
Daniel 6 62
Jonah 1. 64

NEW TESTAMENT REFERENCES

Matthew 2:1-11 68
Matthew 3:1-12 71
Matthew 8:23-27 82
Matthew 14:22-33 85
Matthew 22:15-22 73
Matthew 26:69-75 90
Mark 2:1-12 88
Mark 4:1-20 78
Mark 10:13-16 74
Mark 15:33-41 92
Luke 2:41-52. 69
Luke 19:1-9. 86
Luke 23:33-43. 94
John 1:1-14. 80
John 2:12-25. 76
John 3:16 102
John 3:16-17. 14
John 6:1-14. 84
John 20:24-31. 96
Acts 1:8. 100
Acts 1:1-11 98
Acts 2:1-13 100
Acts 9:1-20 103
Romans 8:38-39 36
1 Corinthians 3:16. 100
Hebrews 11:4 16
Revelation 1:8. 8
Revelation 21:1-7, 16-26; 22:1-3. . . . 105

Theme Index

ATTITUDES

Why Didn't God Like
Cain's Offering?. 16

CREATION

Who Made God? 8
Do I Really Look Like God? 10
Did God Take a Nap on the
Seventh Day?. 12
Did Adam Ever Get His
Rib Back? 14

DREAMS

Do My Dreams Tell the Future
Like Joseph's Dreams Did?. 32

ETERNAL LIFE

Does Jesus Still Have Holes in
His Hands?. 96
Why Is the Book of Revelation
So Confusing? 105

FORGIVENESS
Was God Mad at Moses for
Breaking the Tablets?. 40
Why Did Peter Get Into
So Much Trouble? 90

FRIENDSHIP
Was Jesus More Popular Than
My Favorite Music Group? 88

GIFTS
What Are Frankincense
and Myrrh? 68

GOD'S CONSTANCY
Who Made God? 8
Do My Dreams Tell the Future
Like Joseph's Dreams Did?. 32
Why Did Pharaoh Keep Changing
His Mind About Letting the
Israelites Go? 34

GOD'S LOVE
Why Was Esau So Hairy? 28
Why Didn't Joseph Just
Share His Coat? 30
Why Did God Send All
Those Plagues on Egypt? 36
Was Esther Prettier Than
Snow White? 58
Did Everyone Like Zacchaeus
After He Met Jesus? 86
Why Did Peter Get Into
So Much Trouble? 90

GOD'S POWER
Was Sarah As Old As My Grandma
When She Had Isaac?. 26
Did Goliath Live on
a Beanstalk? 48
Were Shadrach, Meshach,
and Abednego Superheroes? 60

GOD'S PROMISES
Were There Rainbows
Before the Flood?. 20
Was Abram Able to Count
All the Stars? 24
Was Sarah As Old As My Grandma
When She Had Isaac?. 26

Why Did Pharaoh Keep
Changing His Mind About
Letting the Israelites Go?. 34

GOD'S PROTECTION
Did God Take a Nap on
the Seventh Day?. 12
Why Did God Send All Those
Plagues on Egypt? 36
Did Goliath Live on
a Beanstalk?. 48
Did Daniel Get to Pet
the Lions?. 62

GOD'S PROVISION
Did Adam Ever Get His Rib Back? . . . 14
What Did Manna Taste Like?. 38
Did Samson Eat Spinach?. 44
Did the Ravens Bring Toys and
Games to Elijah Too?. 56
Why Did John the Baptist
Eat Such Yucky Food? 71

HEAVEN
Where Is Jesus Now? 98
Why Is the Book of Revelation
So Confusing? 105

HOLY SPIRIT
Where Is Jesus Now? 98
Is the Holy Spirit Inside of Me? 100

JESUS' DEATH AND RESURRECTION
Did God Forget About Jesus
When He Was on the Cross?. 92
Why Didn't Jesus Just Use His
Power to Get Down From
the Cross?. 94
Does Jesus Still Have Holes in
His Hands?. 96

JESUS IS GOD
Was Solomon Smarter Than Jesus? . . 54
Why Were the Pharisees Always
So Mean to Jesus?. 73
If Jesus Liked Children So Much,
Why Didn't He Have Any? 74
Did Jesus Pick Up the Tables After
He Knocked Them Over?. 76
Did Jesus Just Pretend to Be Asleep
Before He Calmed the Storm? 82

Did Jesus Walk on the Moon? 85

Does Jesus Still Have Holes in
His Hands? 96

What Did Jesus Do With All the
Leftover Food After He Fed Five
Thousand People? 84

JESUS' PURPOSE

What Makes Jesus Laugh? 80

If Jesus Liked Children So Much,
Why Didn't He Have Any? 74

Did Jesus Walk on the Moon? 85

Did God Forget About Jesus When
He Was on the Cross? 92

Why Didn't Jesus Just Use
His Power to Get Down
From the Cross? 94

Does Jesus Still Have Holes in
His Hands? 96

OBEDIENCE

Did the Unicorns Miss the Ark? 18

Did the Tower of Babel Go All
the Way to Heaven? 22

Why Did the Israelites March
Around the Wall of Jericho
Seven Times? 42

Why Didn't David Get Even With
Saul When He Had the Chance? . . 52

Did Jonah Get Seasick in
the Whale? 64

PATIENCE

Why Did the Israelites March
Around the Wall of Jericho
Seven Times? 42

PRAYER

Why Can't I Hear God Like
Samuel Did? 46

Did God Forget About Jesus When
He Was on the Cross? 92

SADNESS

Did God Forget About Jesus When
He Was on the Cross? 92

SHARING

What Did Jesus Do With All the
Leftover Food After He Fed Five
Thousand People? 84

SIN

Why Was King Saul
So Grumpy? 50

SPIRITUAL GROWTH

Do I Really Look Like God? 10

Why Can't I Hear God Like
Samuel Did? 46

Was Esther Prettier Than
Snow White? 58

Did Jesus Have to Go to School? 69

Why Did Jesus Tell So
Many Stories? 78

Did Saul's Horses Go
Blind Too? 103

TELLING OTHERS ABOUT GOD

Was Jesus More Popular Than
My Favorite Music Group? 88

Is the Holy Spirit Inside of Me? 100

TRUST

Was Abram Able to Count
All the Stars? 24

Did the Ravens Bring Toys and
Games to Elijah Too? 56

Did Jesus Just Pretend to Be Asleep
Before He Calmed the Storm? 82

Group Publishing, Inc.
Attention: Product Development
P.O. Box 481
Loveland, CO 80539
Fax: (970) 679-4370

Evaluation for
Quick Children's Sermons 4: Did Samson Eat Spinach?

Please help Group Publishing, Inc., continue to provide innovative and useful resources for ministry. Please take a moment to fill out this evaluation and mail or fax it to us. Thanks!

● ● ●

1. As a whole, this book has been (circle one)

not very helpful   very helpful

1   2   3   4   5   6   7   8   9   10

2. The best things about this book:

3. Ways this book could be improved:

4. Things I will change because of this book:

5. Other books I'd like to see Group publish in the future:

6. Would you be interested in field-testing future Group products and giving us your feedback? If so, please fill in the information below:

Name_____

Church Name _____

Denomination _____ Church Size _____

Church Address _____

City _____ State _____ ZIP _____

Church Phone_____

E-mail _____

Creative Resources for Leaders!

Wild & Wacky Bible Lessons on Obedience, Prayer, and Courage: 13 Quick and Easy Lessons for Combined Ages

Featuring Frank Peretti as Mr. Henry

Welcome to the Wild & Wacky World of Mr. Henry (Frank Peretti), the first of four multimedia curriculum kits that will make the Bible come alive for kids of all ages! This one-of-a-kind curriculum kit will be a guaranteed hit with churches of all sizes. It works especially well for combined-age groups and is flexible enough to use in Sunday school, children's church, after school or in midweek programs.

Each Wild & Wacky Bible Lesson Kit contains:

• 3 thirty-minute Wild & Wacky videos containing a total of 6 live-action Bible stories plus animated segments,

• a CD with 7 Bible stories and music,

• a Teacher Guide with 13 complete Bible lessons,

• decoration posters,

• and a fun "gizmo" object lesson.

ISBN 0-7644-2457-2

The Kids' Travel Guide to the Fruit of the Spirit

Take children from K to 5th grade on a life-impacting adventure into the Fruit of the Spirit of Galatians 5:22-23. Engage them with activities, stories, prayer and much more. Children will learn all about the Fruit and how to live them with these 13 power-packed lessons!

ISBN 0-7644-2390-8

Heartfelt Thanks for Sunday School Teachers

How do you truly thank Sunday school teachers in a way that shows deep appreciation, encouragement and inspiration? Give them a *Heartfelt Thanks*! Packed with full-color art, it includes space for journaling and responding to questions. It's great for individual worship and devotional activities. Build up your team members with this perfect gift!

ISBN 0-7644-2433-5